Survive and Thrive
Three Steps to Securing Your Program's Sustainability

By Kylie Hutchinson

National Library of Canada Cataloguing in Publication

Hutchinson, Kylie, 1966 –
        Survive and Thrive: Three Steps to Securing Your Program's Sustainability/Kylie Hutchinson.

ISBN 978-0-9952774-0-3

First edition, 2016

Cover art and book design by Angie Ishak. Illustrations by Angie Ishak & Jana Curll.

Copies of this book may be purchased from www.communitysolutions.ca.

For more information contact:
Kylie Hutchinson
Community Solutions Planning & Evaluation
PO Box 1911
Gibsons, BC, V0N 1V0
Canada
604-243-9458
www.communitysolutions.ca

Acknowledgements

This book was a dream for many years before it finally became a reality. There are many people I wish to thank for helping to make it happen, including:

- Lesley Dyck and Ruth Beck for providing the impetus to learn about program sustainability
- the Center for Civic Partnerships, the Center for Public Health Systems Science at Washington University in St. Louis, and Susan Hailman for granting me permission to adapt and use their worksheets
- Pam Preston, Frank Ritcey, Geetha Van Den Daele, Alex Goss, Kim Leonard, Kathleen Cornett, Sonia Worcel, Adrienne Monks, Tom MacLeod, Janice Duddy, Mike Vanderbeck, Blythe Butler, and Gerry Zipursky for their case study contributions
- Suzanne Doyle-Ingram and Natasha Bailey for giving me gentle pushes when I needed them
- Annaliese Calhoun, Sandra Sellick, Pat Evans, Denise Baker, and Darlene Hope-Ross for reviewing the manuscript
- my husband and daughter for allowing me to disappear every few months to write.

Thank you all.

Table of Contents

Introduction

want to tell you a true story about a friend of mine. Suzanne[1] worked at a small community-based organization with four other colleagues. Her job involved maintaining a large network of collaborative partners who worked on similar issues across the province. She had nurtured and developed this network over a period of five years and saw good things happening. Unfortunately, the organization had only one source of funding which dried up quickly when there was a change in government. The organization responded by giving Suzanne two weeks' notice that they were cutting her hours from five to three days a week. Several weeks later her hours were further reduced to one day a week. She remembers this as a very stressful and uncertain time, both professionally and personally. Because of her commitment to the program and the partnerships supporting it, she tried to squeeze her regular work into fewer days. At the same time, she worried about winding down her job, losing her income, searching for a new job, and most of all, what impact all this would have on her professionally.

> *I worried a lot about the perception of the people I was collaborating with. Since my role was one of the first to be phased out, and so quickly, I worried that people would think I had been fired for something that I did, when really it was the organization's fault for not having a financially sound funding model from the beginning. Given the work that I had to accomplish before the end, there simply wasn't time to speak with everyone I needed to speak with. So for some people, it must have seemed like I just disappeared off the map.*

Perhaps this has never happened to you, but for anyone who is hard-working and dedicated to their job, it's probably one of the worst nightmares possible. In fact, it's estimated that up to 40% of all new social programs do not last long beyond their initial funding.[2] You work hard and are proud of your program, but you wonder if you'll still

---

[1] Not her real name.
[2] Savaya, R., Spiro, S., & and Elran-Barak, R. (2008). Sustainability of social programs: A comparative case study analysis. American Journal of Evaluation, 29, 478-493.

be operating in three years. You want to see your hard-earned efforts sustained, and are concerned about keeping talented staff. Or perhaps you're in the process of planning a new pilot program, and you want to know what you can do to give it the best shot at longevity. If you regularly apply for external funding, you're likely facing direct questions on grant application forms about how you plan to ensure the sustainability of your project. How do you respond?

This book will show you what to say, and what you can do in turn to avoid situations like Suzanne's. In three straightforward steps—Assess, Plan, and Implement—you can begin to create a more sustainable foundation for all your programs and services so you can not only survive, but thrive.

A Bit About Me

I originally started out in the nonprofit sector as a student volunteer and moved on to various paid program coordinator positions. For a short period, I even worked as a fundraiser. Many more years followed as a board member and staff trainer. In my most recent role as an independent consultant, I've worked with clients in the nonprofit, public, and private sectors in numerous areas including health, social services, education, international development, and the environment.

This is me in 1973 repeating the Brownie motto, "Be Prepared." It's a maxim that's equally relevant to sustainability.

For the past eighteen years, I've consulted with nonprofits specializing in the areas of program planning and evaluation. It was through one of these clients that I first became interested in the topic of program sustainability. Fifteen years ago, I worked with a large regional health organization responsible for promoting healthy lifestyles and providing health services to the community. They contacted me because they had recently received one million dollars in funding to launch several innovative health promotion programs in their community. Unfortunately, as with so many grant-funded activities, the programs were only guaranteed this funding for one year, so the organization was naturally concerned about the sustainability of their efforts. Many of these programs involved unique partnerships with community organizations which they didn't want to see end after twelve months. Furthermore, they knew they couldn't achieve their long-term goals with only one year of funding. They asked me, *"Is there anything we can do upfront to ensure our programs get off to the best start possible? When our funding ends, is there some way we can increase their potential for longevity?"*

"Hmm, good question," I thought.

I proceeded to research absolutely everything I could find on program sustainability, both in the academic and non-academic literature. I was truly fascinated by what I found. Researchers working in the area of organizational development examined what happened to programs after their major or seed funding was withdrawn. They compared programs that continued to provide services with those that had been forced to fold, and looked at the differences between the two. I was so excited by what I learned that I wanted to share it with others. After helping this organization, I turned my findings into a face-to-face workshop and online webinar. Over the past thirteen years, I've delivered this training to organizations all over North America. Many of these groups, in turn, were so excited by what they learned that they brought me into their organizations to help them develop a custom program sustainability plan. With this book, I hope I can share that excitement with you.

A Note About Definitions

Definitions are important, and by sustainability, I don't mean the environmental kind. I'm referring to the continuation of a successful program or practice over time. In Chapter 1, I'll explain some important distinctions between types of sustainability, but for now, think of it as your program's long-term viability.

I consider a program to be a set of activities designed to achieve one or more outcomes. For simplicity's sake, I use this term interchangeably with other forms of services and interventions that face sustainability issues, such as projects, strategies, funding streams, and even whole organizations.

For the most part, this guide focuses on the continuation or discontinuation of programs receiving funding from an external agency, as opposed to the sustainability of any outcomes a program might achieve.

Finally, whether you're an organization, agency, institute, department, or whatever, I use those terms interchangeably too.

Who This Book Is For

This book is for everyone who has ever struggled with answering that infamous question encountered on almost every funding application form:

> *What steps are you taking to ensure the sustainability of*
> *this program?*

I'm guessing that up until now you usually answered this question by making up something that sounded intelligent and then you kept your fingers crossed. If you read this book and do the recommended exercises, I promise you will be able to answer this question more confidently (and truthfully). Because program sustainability is not luck. It's the product of a conscientious, step-by-step process. My hope in writing this book is to take what researchers currently know about program sustainability and present it in a brief and user-friendly way. I know what can influence your program's sustainability and I'm thrilled to share it with you, so your programs can not only survive, but thrive.

I've specifically designed this book for people just like you:

- executive directors
- program managers
- front-line staff
- board members
- funders
- people who are passionate about what they do and want to see their initiatives take root and flourish
- people who want to see their hard-won efforts and community impacts last
- busy people who need answers and practical tips fast.

Program sustainability is not luck.

Program sustainability is an issue for all types of organizations: nonprofits, charities, small community groups, foundations, and government. It also applies across all sectors and program areas. No matter what type of program or project you work with, you'll find something of value in this process to help you on your journey towards greater sustainability. Although the content deals primarily with program sustainability, many of the concepts and activities will apply to sustaining small organizations as well.

What's Inside

Inside you'll find thirteen chapters, packed with concrete things you can do to improve your program's sustainability. I have based this book on three simple and straightforward steps:

> **Step 1 - Assess**
> **Step 2 - Plan**
> **Step 3 - Implement**

I've included many real-life case studies from a wide range of programs and practical group activities designed to give you the knowledge and skills you need to keep your services alive.

In Chapters 1 and 2, I define program sustainability and why it's important for agencies like yours. In Chapter 3, I summarize the various factors that the research literature says influences program sustainability. These first three chapters form an important foundation of knowledge that will help you to get the most from the concrete activities that follow.

From here, the focus is on action.

Chapter 4 moves on to look at how and when to begin planning for your program's sustainability. For Step 1 – Assess, Chapters 5 and 6 introduce you to an easy and effective tool for assessing your current sustainability and how to clarify your sustainability goals. For Step 2 – Plan, Chapters 7 through 11 take you through a practical and thought-provoking process for developing your own program sustainability plan. For Step 3 – Implement, Chapter 12 presents an easy to use action plan to help with follow-through. Chapter 13 looks at special considerations for funding bodies, and I close with next steps for moving forward. Since each chapter builds on the one before, I suggest taking your time and going through each chapter in the order presented.

At the end of the book, you'll also find a helpful link to a list of additional resources to continue your learning.

Congratulations!

You're about to take tangible steps towards tackling your program or organization's sustainability. Although there's no magic bullet to solve your funding woes, I do know what influences program sustainability. This book offers concrete research, ideas, and basic steps for you to follow. Armed with this knowledge, you will become a better manager of a better program.

Now is the time to stop worrying about the future and start putting your energy into more effective strategies to improve your program's sustainability. You know you do good work in the community; now you will have the tools to maintain it.

Excited? Let's go!

Learning Objectives

In this chapter, you will learn:

- Three different types of program sustainability.
- Three stages of program sustainability.
- When programs should and shouldn't be sustained.

Chapter I: What is Program Sustainability?

There is no agreed-upon definition of program sustainability. The term has different connotations depending on a program's goals, context, and length of operation. Since it doesn't always mean the same thing to everyone, let's look at three possible sustainability scenarios.

Three Types of Sustainability

Type 1: The continuation of successful pilot programs after major or seed funding is terminated.

This type is familiar to most of us. All too often, it's easy to obtain funding for a new and innovative pilot program, but sustaining all or part of it beyond the original funding period can be a challenge. Even if you've done everything "right", there is no guarantee your funders will re-fund you for the same amount next time. However, many programs can and do survive for years when their funders renew their grants year after year, or if they source new funders each time. It's a risky, but common, model.

Type 2: The transition of a pilot program into a core program within a host agency.

This second type is the goal of many maturing pilot projects: to transition into core operations after demonstrating their effectiveness and worth. Becoming a core program occurs when a host or "backbone" agency housing the pilot recognizes the value that it adds to their own mission. They view the pilot as a good fit, so they decide to give it a more permanent status within their organization. If funders agree, the program continues to receive external funding support, but the host agency fully incorporates it into their operating budget and procedures. However, both the pilot and host agency will adapt in response to changing conditions which may affect this fit over time. Funder priorities and capacity can also change. So again, it's important to note that sustainability is not guaranteed.

Sometimes a program is transferred to a network of agencies that have decided to support it collaboratively. I sometimes call this "spinning off." (The reverse of this would be a pilot intervention that originates from a collaboration but eventually finds a permanent home with one of the partner organizations or the backbone organization.)

Pilot programs are often the source of diffusion of new evidence-based practices, which is common in human service and health care settings. If staff adopt and integrate these new practices into regular operations, this is referred to as uptake, routinization, or institutionalization. However, since the determinants of this type of sustainability are slightly different than for programs, I won't be covering them in detail in this guide.

A More Sustainable Home

The Community Connector Initiative

The Community Connector Initiative is a volunteer bank offering informal support, information, and friendship to newcomers. Grassroots members of the Guelph-Wellington Local Immigration Partnership originally developed the pilot, but organizers knew it would soon need a more secure home. Happily, one was eventually found at the Guelph Neighbourhood Support Coalition (GNSC). Brendan Johnson, Executive Director of the GNSC, says, *"The GNSC is ecstatic to be the home for the Community Connector Initiative. Not only do we get to launch an awesome program, but we get to have a dedicated and passionate team from the Local Immigration Partnership to help us make it happen. The initiative fits perfectly with the GNSC's goals and objectives to support neighbourhoods as places where everyone feels welcome, safe, and at home."* As a bonus, members of the original Local Immigration Partnership have been invited by the GNSC to become advisory group members and continue guiding its development and implementation.

Type 3: The maintenance of program benefits (without the actual program) over the long-term through the development of increased community capacity.

This third type focuses on sustainability at the broader community level. This type of sustainability occurs when a program has been so successful at achieving and maintaining its desired outcomes that it's no longer needed. This is especially true for programs that involve some form of capacity-building within a target population. Understandably, this can be the most challenging form of sustainability to achieve unless you can enshrine your issue as a new policy or legislation. One example is using seat belts. Years ago in North America, many campaigns urged us to wear seat belts when we drive. Nowadays, these are rare. However, in countries where this community capacity is not yet present, such as Zambia, billboards promoting seat belt use regularly dot the landscape.

Remember that these types of sustainability apply not just to programs, but also to projects, policies, and new practices. On a macro level, your organization can have its own broad sustainability issues too. Many people attending my workshops represent small organizations that struggle with sustaining their organization as a whole.

Three Stages of Program Sustainability

You might find it handy to think of these three types of sustainability as stages on a continuum.

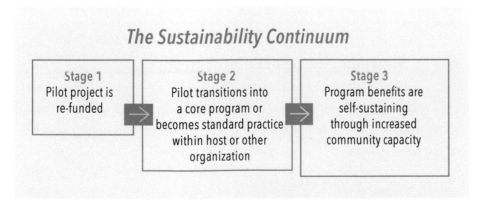

The Sustainability Continuum

| Stage 1 Pilot project is re-funded | Stage 2 Pilot transitions into a core program or becomes standard practice within host or other organization | Stage 3 Program benefits are self-sustaining through increased community capacity |

In Stage 1, a pilot innovation is re-funded and morphs from being a pilot project into a more established program. In Stage 2, it either transitions into a core program or standard practice within the original host or backbone organization or is transferred to a more stable home within another organization or network of organizations. In Stage 3, the program has been operating effectively for so long that community capacity has increased to the point that it's no longer needed and may dissolve. In the final stage, your resources and efforts are better spent elsewhere, as in the seat belts example above.

While we'd all love to be at Stage 3, the reality is that most of us are working hard enough just to reach Stages 1 or 2. Indeed, the majority of programs will remain at these two stages for their entire life cycle. Aside from successes in areas such as seat belts, drinking and driving, and bike helmets, achieving Stage 3 is rare. It does happen, however. In the example opposite, the community of McBride in Northern British Columbia is small enough to provide a glimpse into how it occurs.

Sustainability Goals

What does sustainability look like for your program? What is reasonable to expect for its size, type, age, or design? Is it reaching Stage 1 or 2, or are you aiming for Stage 3? Is it maintaining your services from year to year, or is it scaling up and having a broader reach? Is it a new practice embedded in your organization's daily operations or is it working yourself out of a job? Having a clear sense of your sustainability goals will help as you move forward to develop your sustainability strategies. It's important to keep in mind that total self-sufficiency is a difficult and likely impossible goal for most programs, so be realistic about what you can achieve.

What If Something Shouldn't Be Sustained?

I'm often asked in my workshops and webinars, *"What if something shouldn't be sustained?"* It's true that some programs have a natural endpoint, and we don't want our desire for sustainability to discourage innovation. For years we've been trying to achieve social change, and while some ideas work, a lot of well-intentioned efforts haven't achieved the desired outcomes. If we continue doing the same things year in and year out, we close the door to new ideas and new ways of approaching things. At some point, it's simply better to modify or discontinue an intervention in favour of something more effective.

A Continuum of Sustainability
Northern BC Seniors Falls Prevention Network

When the Northern BC Seniors Falls Prevention Network received three-years of funding from Health Canada and Veterans Affairs, they focused their falls prevention program on two areas: individual falls risk assessment and municipal falls prevention hotlines. In local communities, peer volunteers were trained to conduct in-home falls assessments. When the funding finally ended, they concluded it was not possible to maintain this component without a paid coordinator. However, they were able to achieve a Stage 2 level of sustainability by embedding falls prevention best practices into Northern Health's standard geriatric practices. Nowadays, anyone referred to Community Care in the region receives an initial falls assessment by a case manager, which has also become a standard provincial practice.

The program also piloted several falls prevention hotlines in communities where residents could report falls risk areas in public spaces, such as cracked sidewalks or broken steps. Once a problem area was phoned in, the local municipality went and fixed it. At the end of the funding period, the sustainability of funds to promote these hotlines was in question. For large communities like Prince George, it became the decision of the municipality whether to continue supporting them as a core program or not (Stage 2). But in small communities like the village of McBride (population 582), continuing to promote the hotline was not necessary. Community awareness had increased to the point where residents automatically knew to call the municipality, and they would fix the problem (Stage 3).

I prefer to think of sustainability as a process of maintaining programs (or perhaps only part of a program) that have some evidence supporting their efficacy. As Pam Preston, Executive Director of the Westcoast Child Care Resource Centre, says:

It's hard to stop doing what you've always done. But you have to be really nimble out there. People are trying to hang on for the wrong reasons. You have to ask yourself, 'What's the right thing to do?'. And not for the agency, but for the community. And it may or may not be your program. You have to think bigger about the mission. There may be a loss in that, but that's okay because you can survive the loss and you can change.

I'll talk more about the role program evaluation plays in determining if something should be sustained in Chapter 3.

In this chapter, we've explored how program sustainability can mean different things in different contexts, and how a program can pass through a continuum of sustainability. In the next chapter, we'll look at why focusing on sustainability is important and how it can benefit you and your program.

Chapter 1
SUMMARY

- There are three main types of program sustainability:

  - the continuation of a pilot program after the original funding ends
  - the transition of a pilot program into a core program within a host agency
  - lasting benefits that occur in the absence of the program resulting from greater community capacity.

- Each type falls on a continuum where a program moves through various stages of sustainability. In the first stage, a program typically starts out with pilot status. In Stage 2 it transitions into a core program, then in Stage 3 it eventually dissolves due to a lack of need. The vast majority of programs will remain at the first two stages for their entire life cycle.

- The level of sustainability you aim for will look different depending on the context of your program, so be realistic about what you can achieve.

Learning Objectives

In this chapter, you will learn:

- Twelve reasons why program sustainability is important.

Chapter 2: Why Sustainability is Important

If you truly believe in a program and its benefits, you want to see it survive and thrive. As program staff, you work hard to achieve transformative change in your clients, your community, and the environment. But if your funding comes in fits and starts, or ends just when the program is hitting its stride, the potential to achieve these impacts stops abruptly. This uncertainty not only affects your program; it also hurts your community and society as a whole.

Here are 12 reasons why you should be concerned about your program's sustainability.

Love 'Em and Leave 'Em

It doesn't matter who you serve, how excellent your services are, or how much they love you; your funder will still leave you someday. Yes, it's true that *"Nonprofits depend on funders for support, and funders depend on nonprofits to run programs."*[3] But contrary to popular belief, funders don't have a bottomless pit of money. What they do have is an endless demand for what they do. A well-known author of fundraising manuals once said to me,

> *Where did nonprofits ever get the idea that there is such a thing as core funding? I'm not sure it even exists. No one, including ourselves as individuals, is guaranteed of getting a paycheque every week. Where did nonprofits get the idea that they are any different?*

Yes, your work is effective and yes it is important, but as with many things in life, nothing is forever. It may be painful and unfair, but true. As Suzanne from Chapter 1 said, *"As a team, I think we wrongfully concluded that if we just did good work, the funding would continue and that simply wasn't true."* You may have had the same insight.

---

[3] Le, V. (2015). Why the Sustainability Myth is just as destructive as the Overhead Myth. Retrieved from http://nonprofitwithballs.com/2015/05/why-the-sustainability-myth-is-just-as-destructive-as-the-overhead-myth/#more-2388.

Change Takes Time

Programs don't usually burst out of the gate achieving outcomes. It takes time. Program managers often tell me they spend their first six months (or more) doing things like setting up administration, hiring staff, promoting their services, building trust, recruiting participants, developing partnerships, and so on. In fact, if your program strives to achieve any significant change, it can be at least three to five years before you begin to see impacts. Long-term change does not result from short-term operations. That's why it's important to manage funders' expectations about impact measurement from the outset.

Nothing Is Forever

Eight years ago my husband, an energy engineer, decided to leave private consulting and take a three-year contract position with a nonprofit doing interesting work in his area. His new position was made possible by a sizeable $500,000, three-year grant from Industry Canada. Before this grant, the organization had limped along with only one staff person. With this new funding, they were given the opportunity to ramp up their operations and make a larger impact. Over the next six months, the organization secured formal office space, hired new staff, purchased new computers and other office fixtures, and got down to the business of advancing their mandate. It was an exciting and heady time. But as his spouse, I was concerned about what was going to happen to his paycheque at the end of the three-year grant. I was pretty sure that Industry Canada was not going to give the organization another half million dollars, no matter how good their outcomes were. I told him now was the time to start thinking about how they were going to maintain the new infrastructure they had built and not three months before the funding ran out.

Cost Savings Take Time

Many programs pilot new policies and practices because of the anticipated cost savings they'll produce. But again, these savings can take years to appear. If you wish to realize cost savings, you need to operate over the long term.

Reinventing the Wheel, Again

We don't need research to tell us that terminating programs only to build them up again can be wasteful of resources in the long run. Remember how the first six months of a program is usually spent on administration and start up? Now imagine all this effort being for naught if your program has to fold one year later. Or worse, imagine having to go through a regular cycle of starting up, scaling back, starting up, and scaling back again because of funding insecurities. These ups and downs and the continual re-inventing of the wheel are not only inefficient; they're also disheartening for staff and other stakeholders.

Your Credibility is at Stake

Going to the effort of setting up a program only to dismantle it several years later can breed a dangerous cynicism among the population you serve. Disillusioned participants can become harder to mobilize over time. If you adopt the perspective of taxpayers or donors, you know that the general public can sometimes be skeptical of "new initiatives." Over the years, they've seen their tax dollars poured into new programs only to watch them later fold and disappear, time and time again. This cynicism is dangerous as it not only hampers your ability to obtain community buy-in for new projects, but it also affects your credibility as an organizational overall.

Some Problems Never Go Away

Sustainability will always be a concern for some programs because certain problems will never go away. Think about issues such as youth drinking and driving or safe sex. No matter how effective your interventions are, over time, there will always be a new generation or different target group that needs to hear your message again and again.

Bye Bye Staff

Not surprisingly, one unfortunate by-product of funding instability is the loss of good staff. As much as staff may love working with your program, they have mortgages and expenses themselves to worry about. They can only cling to a sinking ship for so long, and eventually, they have to jump to dry land to save themselves and their families. Even if that ship rights itself later on with new funding, they're likely long gone. This departure may be particularly true of the millennial generation, who show less commitment to staying with an employer over time compared to earlier generations.

The Changing Face of HIV

When HIV/AIDS first surfaced in the early 1980s, the epidemic was largely centred around men who have sex with men (MSM). After a concerted education, prevention, and treatment response, infection rates decreased considerably in this target group. Over time, the epidemic shifted to marginalized and street-involved populations who inject drugs so that by the 1990s, the majority of new infections were diagnosed in an entirely different population. Consequently, attention and resources shifted to address this new priority population. However, as time went by, observers noted that although there was a decline in infection rates among injection drug users, the number of new diagnoses in MSM was once again becoming a concern. Why? The diversion of resources towards injection drug users meant that gay men were not receiving prevention and care services during this time. A new cohort of young gay men emerged that not only failed to receive the same amount of safe-sex education as the previous generation had, but also had not grown up seeing their friends and lovers die during the pre-treatment era of AIDS. Of course, other factors contribute to the current epidemic of HIV among MSM. But from a sustainability perspective, the changing course of the infection and recognition of the complexity of the epidemic among MSM has led internationally to an increased emphasis on renewing this public health response.

Bye Bye Partnerships

Partnerships are a critical aspect of many programs. Many managers tell me that the biggest predictor of a successful collaboration is the personalities of those involved. If one manager knows and trusts her peer at a partner agency on a personal level, that partnership is likely to be more effective and last longer. However, think about what happens if one manager leaves either organization. All the time spent building a trusting relationship goes out the door with that manager, possibly placing the partnership at risk. Or new efforts and resources have to be applied to building a new personal relationship with new players.

Bye Bye Organizational Memory

When staff leave, you lose a lot more than just talent. Since 90% of the knowledge in an organization is tacit[4], consider this. When staff go out the door, a part of your organizational memory leaves with them. Your staff carry an immense amount of knowledge about the program and its history in their heads. This information is critical for the program to move forward efficiently and effectively.

---

[4] Wah, L. (1999). Making knowledge stick. In Management Review (pp. 24-29). New York, NY: American Management Association International.

All Hands on Deck

Dealing with a sustainability crisis can significantly drain your organization's reserves in the short-term. If you're already concerned about sustainability, you might not have the capacity to deal with these sorts of emergencies too often.

Code Red Years ago, I volunteered on the board of a large multi-service organization that operated a much needed early child care program in my community. One day the director of this program received word from their primary funder that they were about to lose a significant amount of funding, which would essentially force them to close. Believing that the program provided a critical service to parents in the community, the organization quickly drafted a plan of action to save it. Over a period of several weeks, they:

- held planning meetings with other similarly threatened programs
- distributed posters and flyers at parent activities
- prepared press releases

- met with their elected provincial and federal representatives
- coordinated a town hall meeting
- held a local march
- traveled to a large rally in the provincial capital

As you can imagine, all this activity took a lot of time and energy away from the organization's other regular services. Although the staff were successful in reinstating the funding, the toll on the organization was significant. Because the program was so small, it was forced to draw on the help of staff from other programs in the organization to carry out the immense task facing them. Various staff were drawn away from their regular duties for several weeks. The organization also "spent" a good deal of its social capital by calling on the support of its allies, which can't be done that often. In the end, it was worth it, but it took time before everyone felt back on track.

Don't Touch My Program

Sustainability research tells us that programs with strong community connections and feelings of "ownership" are more likely to stick around than those without. But cultivating this level of community ownership takes time. A lot of time in fact, and certainly more than most funding arrangements provide.

Stuck in Pilot Mode

Do your long-term strategic goals ever feel like a target that continually moves farther and farther into the distance? It doesn't help when you have to reduce or cease your operations due to funding cuts, only to turn around and ramp everything up again a short time later. These disruptions can have a "one step forward, two steps backward" effect on your ability to meet your long-range goals. You might dutifully go through a regular strategic planning process, but if you're not able to sustain your services, how can you begin to tackle your long-term agenda? You may end up stuck in pilot project mode, never moving beyond the short term.

So What Are the Benefits of Sustainability?

Let's consider all these negative impacts again, but this time in a positive light. Take a look at the two programs on the next page. Which one would you prefer to be?
I'm sure you'll agree that Program B looks a lot more attractive. Sustainability is critical to the success of many programs.

Program A		Program B
constantly writes grant proposals		writes occasional grant proposals
stuck on short-term outcomes		makes progress on intermediate and long-term outcomes
high staff turnover		
weak organizational memory		stable and talented staff
staff time spent on program start-up and fundraising	VS.	strong organizational memory
		staff time spent on advancing mission
continually re-inventing the wheel		able to fine tune activities over time
short-term labour-intensive partnerships		long-term beneficial partnerships
evidence of program efficiency		evidence of program effectiveness
funding with strings attached		funding with no strings attached
low credibility with stakeholders		high credibility with stakeholders

While Program B may seem like a distant dream, let's explore some tangible ways you can work towards making it a reality for your program. In the next chapter, we'll begin to look at what makes a program more resilient and sustainable.

Chapter 2
SUMMARY

- There are many compelling reasons to ensure your effective programs are sustained over time. Beyond the continuous provision of service, long-term sustainability can impact your organizational efficiency and effectiveness, stakeholder credibility, human resources, and partnerships.

- A lack of sustainability can impede your overall mission advancement and long-term change in our communities and society as a whole.

Learning Objectives

In this chapter, you will learn:

- Common factors related to program sustainability.

Consider

Why do some organizations or their programs die while others continue successfully for decades? Think about an organization or program you know of that's been around for many years. It could be something like the Girl Guides or Boy Scouts, the YMCA, or perhaps Greenpeace. What is it about this organization that you think contributes to its long-term sustainability?

Chapter 3: What Influences Program Sustainability?

What Does Research Tell Us About Sustainability?

When I first started investigating this area, I was delighted to see that other researchers had the same interest in learning more about what makes a program sustainable. Some of the studies I read (see Bibliography) had retrospectively examined one or more programs in depth to determine what was influencing their longevity. Others compared programs that had operated continuously for years with those that had to fold when their major or seed funding was withdrawn. What they discovered was very compelling. They observed distinct differences in how these programs operated and their infrastructure, many of which were associated with increased durability.

It's important to note that this research is relatively nascent, and rigorous study is still needed. While some factors were identified as predictors, others were only correlated with sustainability. In other words, even though a factor is associated with longevity, there isn't necessarily a cause and effect relationship. Indeed, sustainability most likely arises out of complex interactions between these factors and other aspects of the system surrounding your program. Nevertheless, it's intriguing to learn what these characteristics are and to see which ones surface again and again in unrelated studies. Having a solid awareness of them is the first step towards developing a rational sustainability action plan. Best of all, you don't need to read all these studies yourself because I've conveniently condensed these factors into an easy-to-read table for you.

The Challenges of Researching Sustainability

Sustainability researchers face several hurdles when answering the question of what makes a program sustainable. Some of these methodological challenges include:

- varying conceptualizations of sustainability in different sectors
- lack of agreement on what it means for a program to be "sustained"
- comparing different types of programs across different sectors and widely varying contexts
- few empirical studies, with findings often based on retrospective descriptive studies
- potential biases in self-reported data
- lack of standardized, rigorous measurement tools and robust analysis
- little long-term follow-up of "sustained" programs.

In fact, researchers acknowledge they still know very little about the conditions under which new program innovations are sustained. While sustainability is likely the combination of a variety of factors that interact with the complex system that surrounds a program, we don't exactly know how these factors interact or how this impacts sustainability. Since much of this research has focused on health care practices and public health programs, we also don't know if these factors vary across different populations, settings, issue areas, and types of programs. However, I'm excited by the potential of what we can achieve with what we currently know.

Primary Factors Influencing Program Sustainability

Although researchers have not identified a uniform set of factors across diverse programs, some are identified more frequently in studies than others. I have summarized what I believe to be the most relevant for nonprofits in the following table.

Consider

As you're reading each factor, consider how it applies to your current situation. Are there any that you can enhance to increase your overall sustainability? Note that not all factors will be relevant to your particular situation. Depending on the type of program and context, some factors may be more influential than others. But the earlier you can focus on these, the better you can position yourself for greater sustainability.

28 Factors That Influence the Sustainability of Programs

FUNDING
- External Funding Environment
- Diverse Sources of Funding
- Sufficient Start-up Resources
- Multi-year Funding
- Realistic Program Budget
- Significant In-kind Resources

PLANNING & EVALUATION
- A Sustainability Plan
- Demonstrated Worth & Value

PROGRAM DESIGN
- Responds to a Clear Need
- Evidence-informed
- Clear Vision and Goals
- Community-driven
- Local Values and Culture
- Volunteer Delivery
- Flexibility and Adaptability
- Strategic Dissemination
- Transition to Policy

PARTNERS
- Collaborative Partners
- Program Champions

PERSONNEL
- Strong & Continuous Leadership
- Local Program Staff
- Engaged Funders

HOST AGENCY
- Fit with Host Agency
- Host Agency Capacity

COMMUNITY
- Strong Community Support
- Local Government, Policy Maker & Business Support

COMMUNICATIONS
- High Visibility
- Strategic Communications

Survive and Thrive: Three Steps to Securing Your Program's Sustainability.
Copyright © 2016 by Kylie S. Hutchinson.
www.communitysolutions.ca.

Derived from: Bracht et al. (1994); Center for Civic Partnerships (2001); Centre for Community Leadership & Grantham (2000); Coalition for Community Schools (2003); Duplechain (2001); Evashwick & Ory (2003); Foreman et al. (2001); Goodman & Steckler (1989); Goodman et al. (1993); Hailman (2001); Holder & Moore (2000); Jackson et al. (1994); Marek et al. (1999, 2003); Paine-Andrews (2000); Rosenheck, (2001); Shediac-Rizhallah & Bone (1998); Scheirer (2005); Scheirer & Dearing (2011); Schell et al. (2013); Smith et al. (1993); Stirman et al. (2012); The Finance Project (2002); Victorian Government Department of Human Services (2001), Whelan et al. (2014).

Funding

External Funding Environment

Having an adequate revenue stream remains a primary and obvious factor affecting the long-term viability of your program. This itself depends on the political and economic climate and if there is a favorable funding environment. Support from decision-makers at various levels of government is important too because they hold the purse strings for public grant dollars. But securing external funding is not the only thing you can do. Read on!

Diverse Sources of Funding

Having only one source of funding is like keeping all your funding "eggs" in one basket and can leave you extremely vulnerable. Why? Imagine that your program is a table held up by four different sources of revenue. If one of those sources were to dry up, you wouldn't tip over because you've still got three legs for support. This is similar to what financial planners have been telling us for years; be sure to have a diversified investment portfolio or in this case, diversified revenue.

What does diversified revenue look like? Often folks in my workshops will describe three or four different grants they receive, but remember that grants are only one source of funding. There's a whole array of different revenue sources for organizations to tap into including:

• individual donations	• corporate donations
• major gifts	• corporate sponsorship
• planned giving	• community foundations
• fee for service	• charitable gaming or gambling
• in-kind contributions	• membership fees
• partnerships	• investment income
• social enterprises	• special events

If you're a small organization with limited capacity and accustomed to only applying for grants, I recognize that this can be quite an intimidating leap for you. Even larger organizations struggle to establish and manage funding initiatives such as individual donor programs and labour intensive social enterprises. But if you can start small and persevere, the payoff can be

A Four-legged Table

Campbell River and District Association for Community Living

One example of an organization with diversified revenue is the Campbell River and District Association for Community Living (CRADACL). CRADACL's mission is to provide and advocate for local services to support people of all ages with special needs, their families, and caregivers. The association is more than fifty years old, which might explain the diversity of revenue sources they have developed over time including:

- provincial government contracts
- provincial and federal grants
- four social enterprises:
  - Skyline Productions Wood Products
  - Skyline Productions Confidential Paper Shredding
  - Scan Now
  - Community Living College (which trains and certifies community support workers)
- rental income from several social housing units
- individual and corporate donations
- in-kind donations
- special events

Although CRADACL still struggles like many organizations to meet the demand for their service, their four-legged table won't be tipping anytime soon.

immense for your sustainability. Not only will you have more stable legs for your table, but those legs may come in the form of unrestricted funding. Many grants and government contracts come with strings attached: who, where, how, and when you can spend the money. Conversely, unrestricted funding from sources such as fee-for-service or individual donors has relatively few limitations. You are free to allocate it exactly where you know it will best serve your community or issue. Remember in Chapter 2 when I said there's no such thing as core funding? Unrestricted funding is as close as you can get. Whichever of these revenue sources you decide to pursue, you will need to do your homework beforehand to ensure it's right for your organization and worth the investment of time and resources.

While this book isn't intended to be a detailed fundraising guide, I also don't want to make light of what can be a major undertaking for you and your program. Diversifying your revenue is not a quick fix if you're struggling. It's an important but long-haul change that begins with the first step

Some forms of revenue come with more strings and vulnerabilities than others. Think about the typical expectations and accountability that comes with government contracts or foundation grants. Now think about all the ways you might use unrestricted funds to further your mission. Consider also how easily government contracts and foundation grants can disappear. Revenue sources such as individual donations and earned income can provide more security and more importantly, the freedom to use the funds where you know they are needed most.

Show Me the Money

Sources of Canadian not-for-profit revenue, 2008

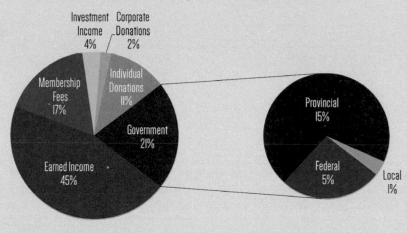

Excludes hospitals and educational institutions.

Statistics Canada. (2010). Satellite Account of Nonprofit Institutions & Volunteering.

Individual Donations

In 2008, Statistics Canada examined sources of revenue for nonprofits in Canada. Although dated, I believe these findings hold some interesting lessons from a sustainability perspective. Looking at the chart above, you might be surprised to learn that earned income, membership fees, and individual donations have provided a far bigger revenue source than what government, foundations, and corporate sponsorships typically offer on average (when hospitals and educational institutions are excluded). These are great examples of unrestricted revenue.

Earned Income

Between one-half to three-quarters of Canadian charities engage in some form of earned income-generating activity, and most of these engage in more than one. Fee for service initiatives and product sales are just two examples of earned income. Depending on the size of the charity, the funds produced from this earned income can account for as much as half of their total revenue on average.

The point I want to make here is that unrestricted funding is better sustainability-wise and individual donations and earned income are great sources of unrestricted funds. So when you think about diversifying your revenue, think about where the money is. Or more specifically, where greater security and freedom are.

of adopting a broader view and a more entrepreneurial spirit in seeking alternative sources of revenue.

Sufficient Start-up Resources

Just like plants and children, your pilot programs need a minimum level of resources to ensure they get the best start possible. When a program has the resources they need to cover their true overhead, they can function better and make an impact. Many organizations and programs operate at a deficit unknowingly because they don't fully understand their program expenses. Programs that are starved from the beginning can be challenged to meet the threshold for success.

Adopting an Entrepreneurial Approach

Safe Spaces: Bullying Education Prevention for Young Children

Safe Spaces is a pro-social program operated by the Westcoast Child Care Resource Centre that teaches young children the skills they need to resist and prevent bullying. The original program model provided training and a kit for child care providers, but after ten years of operation, the program found itself facing several delivery challenges and an uncertain future. Following a series of consultations with key informants, it was clear the program needed a serious re-think to become more sustainable. Staff adopted an entrepreneurial approach and restructured the curriculum by dropping the kit component and redesigning the training course to be a stand-alone fee-for-service product for purchase by other trainers across the province. This move effectively saved the program. In fact, it was so successful they've also taken the same approach with their Responsible Adult Course for those working in school-age child care settings.

Multi-year Funding

Funders take note! Programs with longer funding horizons of three to five years have more breathing room to build their capacity for sustainability than those with only one year.

Realistic Program Budget

While a new pilot program needs sufficient start-up resources, it also needs to be thrifty. This thriftiness is similar to the concept of saving for a rainy day or "bootstrapping" as they call it in new business start-ups. Bootstrapping is the practice of stretching your resources as far as you can until funding is more stable. Resist the urge to purchase new computers, office furniture, and other non-essential supplies. The money you save might be what helps you through your first funding shortfall.

Significant In-kind Resources

In-kind resources are donations of supplies or services instead of cash. Items such as office space, a photocopier, food, vehicles, or volunteers are all in-kind resources. Even volunteers are considered to be in-kind. While some companies or groups may not be able to write you a cheque, they will gladly give you something tangible such as printing services or a few pro bono hours of a professional's time. These in-kind resources can be particularly helpful in getting through famine periods.

Weathering Hard Times with In-kind Resources

WISH Drop-in Centre Society

For several years in the nineties, I served as a volunteer board member of WISH, a drop-in centre for sex workers. At times, being on the board felt like riding a funding roller coaster. Occasionally, a wealthy businessperson would walk in the door, and spontaneously write us a cheque for $60,000. *"Hooray!"* we'd say, and extend our opening hours to seven days a week and hire more part-time staff. Things would go well for several months until we spent all the money. Then we would have to go back to closing on weekends. A few months later, we would get a cheque for $25,000 from a local church group which allowed us to open one more night a week. For many years we continued this way, up and down, down and up, always seeming to court financial disaster. But we never had to shut the doors. Why? I believe it was because of the high levels of in-kind support. This support included a large corps of volunteers, which meant we could function with a skeleton crew of paid staff until more funds came in. For many years, services were also located in a space donated by a local church and we received all of our food via donation. So when times were tough, WISH could tough it out. WISH was a classic example of a program that regularly goes through a feast and famine cycle. Sometimes the funding is abundant; sometimes it's not. But rather than folding, we were able to hunker down and weather the hard times, much like a seed over winter. Our in-kind resources acted like a protective coating to help us survive until conditions changed, and we could flourish again. You'll see this concept illustrated over and over again in our discussions about sustainability. Today, WISH is a strong and thriving organization. But they still recognize the role of in-kind donations in their overall sustainability.

Planning & Evaluation

A Sustainability Plan

Remember Suzanne from Chapter 1? In retrospect, Suzanne says she would have spent a bit more time developing a sustainability plan to address their vulnerability in having only one funding source. I find it curious that although many organizations diligently develop a strategic plan, few seem to draft a sustainability plan. A sustainability plan is a conscious response to the fearful dilemma of what to do when your funding runs out. Programs with managers who have taken the time to develop a formal sustainability plan can increase their potential to continue over the long term. One US study that examined 94 defunct youth programs found that only two had developed a sustainability plan.[5] An ideal sustainability plan is one that you develop at the beginning of your program, includes multiple strategies, and becomes a part of your overall strategic plan. In Chapter 4, I'll introduce you to a basic three-step system you can use to make it a straightforward and engaging process for you, your staff, and your stakeholders.

Although many organizations diligently develop a strategic plan, few seem to draft a sustainability plan.

Demonstrated Worth and Value

Here's an important finding from the research: programs that have undergone a relatively recent outcome evaluation tend to demonstrate greater sustainability than those that haven't. When you have evidence that documents the impact of your program you are better able to present a more compelling rationale to funding bodies, both old and new. Being able to demonstrate your worth formally is a very strong factor in greater sustainability. Having a solid monitoring and evaluation plan in place ensures your program is being delivered effectively and efficiently and merits continuation.

[5] Marek, L. I., Mancini, J. A., & Brock, D. (1999). Continuity, success, and survival of community-based projects: The national youth at risk program sustainability study. Petersburg, VA: Virginia Cooperative Extension.

Evaluation 101:
A Primer on Demonstrating Your Worth

Many of you will already be familiar with the term "program evaluation." If you're not, here's a popular definition:

> Program evaluation is the systematic collection and analysis of information about program activities, characteristics, and outcomes to make judgments about the program, improve program effectiveness, and/or inform decisions about future programming.[6]

The following is a simple overview of the two most common types of evaluation you'll encounter.

Process Evaluation

A process evaluation (also called formative evaluation) focuses on how your program is being implemented and operates. It ensures that your program remains on track to achieve later outcomes.

A process evaluation answers questions such as:

- Are we providing services as intended?
- What is working well and not working well with our services?
- Are we reaching our target market?
- Are participants satisfied with the program?
- What else could or should we be doing?

Outcome Evaluation

An outcome evaluation (also called summative evaluation) determines what outcomes and impacts have occurred as a result of your program. Outcomes are benefits or changes as a result of your program's activities.

It answers questions such as:

- Was the program effective?
- What difference did it make?
- Do our outcomes differ across different sites?
- Was it worth it given the overall time and resources invested?

Most programs already do a lot of process evaluation. They're comfortable collecting

cont'd

---

[6] Patton, M. Q. (1997). Utilization-focused evaluation. Thousand Oaks, CA: Sage.

operational statistics to make sure their service delivery is on track. It's outcome evaluation where many programs typically struggle, and for good reason. Good outcome evaluation requires additional time, resources, and expertise that some organizations simply don't have. Many program managers try to do it off the side of their desk, and this can be challenging.

So what can you do? First of all, it's not necessary to crank out a large outcome evaluation every year. The shelf life of a good quality outcome evaluation can be quite long. In my experience, organizations that manage to conduct a relatively comprehensive and high-quality outcome evaluation can use the results for several years afterward.

Here are several other ideas for getting an outcome evaluation done on a limited budget:

- Don't assume you need to hire an expensive consultant to conduct the whole evaluation. Many evaluation consultants are happy to mentor or coach staff several hours a month through the evaluation process.

- Determine which aspects of the evaluation you or your staff can do yourselves, and which you should contract out to a professional. For example, you might need a consultant's help to develop the evaluation plan, but you might be able to administer an anonymous survey to clients yourself. You might be able to collate and analyze your program records yourself, but it's preferable to have an external evaluator conduct the interviews and focus groups.

- Find a graduate student who might be interested in evaluating your program for their thesis.

- Hire a summer student to complete smaller-sized evaluations.

- Find a skilled volunteer or knowledge philanthropist who will assist you pro bono.

- If you have based your program design on a particular model, see what other evaluations you can find in the research literature and use this as proxy evidence. Although the context may be slightly different, it's possible that someone has conducted a controlled study on your program model or topic area, saving you valuable time and resources. If you need help with this, ask a post-secondary student for assistance.

Whatever you do, it's good to start adopting the common practice of allocating at least 10% of your program budget towards evaluation, before the program begins.

Reusable Results

Immigrant Services
Society of BC

Years ago, I coordinated an employment training program for the Immigrant Services Society of BC. We trained Canadian newcomers on income assistance to be home care aides. When I started, the program had been in operation for ten years. I was curious about where graduates had ended up, and although our funder didn't ask for it, I decided to conduct my own informal outcome evaluation. I spent several weeks tracking down approximately sixty former students to see where they had landed. I wanted to know if they were working as home care aides, if they had other jobs, or if they were they back on income assistance. The results were amazing. Ten years later, approximately 80% of graduates were still working, and the majority of these were home care aides. A few had moved on to higher earning jobs working as residential care attendants. I took these results and summarized them in a simple two-page report. For the next three years when funding proposals were due, I would staple this report to the end of every grant application I prepared. Since the results were so impressive, I was able to re-use them over and over and over again. The funder was thrilled, and we continued to receive our funding for another three years.

Program Design

Responds to a Clear Need

Programs with a clearly recognized need and on-going demand tend to stick around longer than those that don't. I once worked with a rural HIV organization. They regularly struggled with getting their community to accept the fact that there were people in their town with HIV/AIDS. One of their first sustainability strategies was to convince their community that HIV was a serious problem. Other programs work with target populations that continually turn over and create an ongoing demand. For example, youth participants eventually "age out" of youth programs and move on, only to be replaced by a new set of youth who need exposure to the same intervention or message. These types of programs can present a compelling argument for their need to continue.

Evidence-informed

Programs that are based on evidence-informed practices or aligned in some way with a credible institution are also associated with greater sustainability. This association can range from a partnership with a university to using a program model endorsed by a respected institution in the field, for example, the Mayo Clinic. While it's not entirely clear why, it may be that the program has a greater potential to achieve significant outcomes.

Are We Making a Difference? Westcoast Child Care Resource Centre	When the Westcoast Child Care Resource Centre lost fifty-percent of their funding, Executive Director, Pam Preston, became very interested in program sustainability. Pam remembers receiving news of the cut as, *"…shocking and unexpected, as we lost 25 positions with only six weeks' notice."* She recalls, *"It fundamentally changed how the programs had to function. We had to let go of much of what we used to do. We were unionized, so we had to re-write staff job descriptions and totally re-vision what work they were going to be able to do under the new funding scenario. Then we had to post the jobs, interview, and hire them in the new job descriptions."* During this process, eight staff got so frustrated they did not compete for the new positions and decided to leave the agency permanently, which she recalls as *"really tragic."* Nowadays, Pam feels they're doing a lot of things differently, one of which is being more attentive to evaluating their outcomes and demonstrating their worth. *"Now we will look at new projects or existing projects, and say, 'What difference are they making? Do they align with our vision, mission, and values?' If we can't identify significant outcomes, then it's time to think differently. You have to ask yourself, if you can't prove that it's making a difference, then why are you doing it?"*

Clear Vision and Goals

Have you ever encountered an organization or a program that wasn't entirely clear on what they were trying to accomplish? Having a crystal-clear vision and goals that are easily understood by all makes it easier for stakeholders to understand and support your program. But it's not just about clarity. Continuity in your vision and goals will also go a long way towards building the community profile and goodwill you need for people to support you over the long term.

Community-driven

Sustainability research tells us that programs with grassroots support are also more likely to last longer. Grassroots support means community members have requested or initiated a program themselves versus taking on one that funders or experts have offered or imposed upon a community. Think of a bottom-up versus top-down scenario, where community residents and service providers collectively say, *"We see this as an important need in our community, and we're willing to support it."* This early community commitment and support[7] can give a new program a major sustainability advantage over top-down delivered ones.

Bottoms-up Prince George Council of Seniors	When Health Canada and Veterans Affairs Canada announced funds to address the issue of falls prevention, local seniors groups in Northern BC were ready. Northern Health, the regional health service provider, already had seniors advisory committees in local communities that provided input into health care issues. Local groups like the Prince George Council of Seniors knew there was a problem with falls because they had already surveyed seniors' health needs across their region. When federal agencies announced funding, seniors across Northern BC were already well aware of the issue and had a significant willingness to address it.

Local Values and Culture

Another factor that appears to promote greater sustainability is the ability of a program to reflect local community values and culture. Although the exact mechanism isn't clear, it may be that these types of programs are more community-driven and better able to develop community ownership.

[7] In Chapter 8 you can see a good example of this in the North Okanagan Falls Prevention Program case study.

Weaving Local Culture into Program Design

Aboriginal Head Start in Urban and Northern Communities

The Aboriginal Head Start in Urban and Northern Communities Program (AHSUNC) is an initiative of the Public Health Agency of Canada designed to reach vulnerable populations of Aboriginal children at risk for poor early childhood development outcomes. AHSUNC projects are typically preschool programs for children aged three to five years old. The program began in 1995 and has continued to receive funding over the past twenty years. One likely factor in AHSUNC's sustainability is the ongoing need it addresses. In 2012, there were approximately 47,910 Aboriginal children aged three to five years in Canada, of which only 10% were reached annually through AHSUNC. But another driver of sustainability is the requirement for all programs to be locally designed and managed. The program weaves Aboriginal culture and language throughout the design and delivery of the program. There is a strong emphasis on parental involvement in the program and project staff are hired from within each Aboriginal community as much as possible. Some project sites have become known as the community "hub," creating a sense of community for Aboriginal children and their families. Their longevity appears to be paying off. A large federal evaluation of the program concluded that the program has a positive effect on school readiness, specifically in improving children's language, social, motor and academic skills, and cultural literacy.

Volunteer Delivery

Programs that can use volunteers or peers for delivering certain aspects of their service are considered more resilient during periods of funding instability. Volunteers can continue to provide services even though paid employees or the full program structure might not be in place. If a program needs to cut back on paid staff, sometimes it is possible for trained volunteers to continue delivering services, albeit in a limited fashion, until funding improves. One early study of sustainability found that programs that can be delivered in the absence of paid staff have a four times greater likelihood of being maintained over time.[8]

Because It's What I Do

Peer Educator Harm Reduction Program

The power of a peer delivery model to foster program sustainability was revealed to me one day when I was conducting an evaluation of a street nurse peer outreach program. For two years, inner city street nurses used trained peer educators to enhance their HIV and sexually-transmitted infection prevention and education work on the street. The program hired peer educators on short-term contract for six to eight hours a week. They were responsible for assisting with various harm reduction services including needle exchange, wound care, and basic health education. However, after two years funding for the peer educators ended. As the program evaluator, one of my tasks was to interview each peer educator. By the time this occurred, eight months had passed since they had received their last paycheque. I was struck by the number who showed up still carrying their "Peer Educator"-labelled backpack filled with health education pamphlets, clean syringes, and basic first aid supplies. When I asked them why they were still carrying the backpack even though their contract had finished, several replied, *"Because it's what I do."* The positive self-esteem that resulted from being a peer educator was enough to motivate them to remain in their role whether there was funding to pay them or not. They didn't mind continuing because it made them feel good. The implications of this can be huge for program sustainability. When a program receives notice of funding cutbacks and needs to reduce their paid staff, it may be possible for trained volunteers to continue delivering services, albeit in a limited fashion, until funding improves.

[8] O'Loughlin, J., L. Renaud, L. Richard, L. S. Gomez, and G. Paradis. (1998). Correlates of the sustainability of community-based heart health promotion intervention. Preventive Medicine, 27, 702-12.

Flexibility and Adaptability

Flexibility and adaptation are necessary for a program to survive. Programs with the ability to adapt to changing social, economic and political trends, or newly emerging evidence or practices, are more likely to continue over the long term. In fact, most programs evolve over time to adapt to their context and meet the needs of their participants. While fidelity to a prescribed model or the original program proposal is necessary in some circumstances, it's not always desirable as this can stifle innovation. Consider veterans' organizations such as The War Amps. If they only supported veterans, would they still be around today? When the Massachusetts-based Communities That Care Coalition was concerned about their sustainability they expanded their focus to include nutrition and physical activity in addition to their original focus on substance use prevention. However, you also need to be wary of being too flexible. This is a danger when faced with the temptation of adapting to external funder priorities that stray outside of your own program's mandate, which is also known as "mission creep."

Evolve or Die

Bear Aware

Bear Aware was a program that worked with individual communities to reduce the frequency and intensity of human-bear conflicts. The program included components on public education, managing bear attractants, implementing and enforcing bear-smart bylaws, and facilitating community-wide bear-smart planning. However, when a new Provincial Coordinator, Frank Ritcey, took over, it was clear that the need for their services was changing. There were sharp increases in conflicts with additional types of wildlife, including coyotes and deer, and the number of groups approaching the government to deal with these conflicts was increasing as well. To keep their services relevant, Bear Aware decided to expand their mandate to deal with all types of human-wildlife conflict and transition into WildSafe-BC. Ritcey says, *"We realized that Bear Aware needed to grow with the times. It was a matter of staying relevant. You either had to expand or die."* He also notes that *"It was difficult because everyone's entrenched. Bear Aware had a really good public reputation and brand awareness, but we had to do it."* Before the transition, Bear Aware was very focused on homeowners. One benefit of their new mandate is they are now working with different stakeholders and issues that have allowed them to access new funding sources. For example, they are currently working with farmers and orchardists to show them how to grow crops in a manner that minimizes the potential for conflict with wildlife. This new direction has made them eligible for funding from Agriculture Canada, which they would not have had access to before. Similarly, their work with urban deer issues has attracted the attention of the Union of BC Municipalities (UBCM). *"We've developed a strong relationship with the UBCM now and work in partnership with them as we deal with the always difficult issue of urban deer. That really strengthens our case when we seek out more funding to expand our deer programming."* Ritcey believes they're in a much stronger position now regarding their sustainability. He says, *"When I started we had only two years of funding ahead of us. But now it's been growing ever since. Last year our funding was the highest it's ever been, and this year we'll probably top that. That's in direct response to our increased ability to deliver on other wildlife."*

Strategic Dissemination

Broader dissemination is often a goal of pilot projects. If a project proves to be effective, there is a desire to scale it up so it can have a greater impact. However, the sustainability of new sites is not always guaranteed. The McConnell Foundation has examined this area in depth and likens the dissemination of pilot programs to planting a seed.[9] The seed that does well in one type of soil is not guaranteed to sprout and flourish in another location if it does not have the same weather conditions, soil quality, or level of care. It's the same with disseminating a program. If you intend to scale up a successful innovation for the long-term, take care to investigate the conditions of the new sites to ensure you have the best conditions possible for growth and longevity.

Transition to Policy

If there were an ultimate sustainability goal for your program, it would likely be transitioning to formal policy. In Chapter 1, we discussed the final stage of sustainability as the long-term maintenance of program benefits through the development of increased community capacity. When you can turn your intervention into some form of policy, bylaw, or legislation, it becomes a matter of compliance. Ideally, depending on monitoring and enforcement, the need for your intervention will slowly disappear. Consider bike helmet use in the province of British Columbia. Before 1995, many injury prevention programs urged us to wear a helmet. Nowadays, wearing one has become a social norm, and drastically fewer public health resources are spent in this area. It's the same with smoking restrictions and tobacco use. Many studies have found that smokefree bylaws and policies reduce tobacco use, decreasing the use of public funds in smoking cessation and prevention programs.[10]

Partners

Collaborative Partners

Collaboration and partnerships also play a significant role in fostering your program's sustainability. Although stand-alone programs can be eas-

[9] J. W. McConnell Family Foundation. (1998). Should you sow what you know? The Foundation's primer for those developing, or referring, an applied dissemination proposal. Montreal, PQ: J. W. McConnell Family Foundation.
[10] Centre for Disease Control. Smokefree policies reduce smoking. Retrieved from http://www.cdc.gov/tobacco/data_statistics/fact_sheets/secondhand_smoke/protection/reduce_smoking/.

ier to implement and manage, they are harder to sustain over the long term. Again, think of your program as a four-legged table with each leg being a partner organization. Each partner contributes something, such as funding, operational support, or volunteers. If there are funding cutbacks and one partner needs to pull out, your program will not tip over because of the support of the other three partners. Time and again, this factor surfaces as a very significant element of sustainability. Partnering is not always easy, but there are lots of resources online about how to structure a collaboration for the best outcomes.

Sustaining Your Collective Impact

Collaboration and coalitions aren't new in the non-profit sector, but the term "Collective Impact" certainly is. Collective Impact (CI) is a form of partnership that involves diverse community groups adopting a common strategy to solve complex social problems. The five precursor conditions to a successful CI initiative are a common agenda, mutually-reinforcing activities, shared measurement, continuous communication, and a backbone structure. Many of the 28 factors that promote program sustainability apply to a CI scenario as well. Clear vision and goals, strong and competent leadership, multi-year funding, responding to a clear need, community driven, program champions, and engaged funders can all go a long way to seeing your CI project maintained over time.

Important to CI, however, is the need to sustain momentum. In my experience, large-scale collaborative initiatives usually start off with a bang, but can sometimes struggle to maintain their enthusiasm and relevancy over time. Here are six additional tips for sustaining your Collective Impact collaborative.

Ensure a Strong Backbone
A strong backbone organization is one that has the stability and internal capacity to not only provide continuity over time but also encourage forward movement if CI members become distracted by their own agency-specific issues.

cont'd

Early Wins

Early wins are instrumental for demonstrating the potential of the collaborative to members and can further reinforce their resolve to participate. These successes can also serve as a touchstone to remind members of the power of the collaborative if interest is flagging.

Continuous Leadership

While visionary and dynamic leadership is critical for CI to be successful, continuity is also important. CI initiatives usually address complex social issues that are difficult to fix in the short-term. Having a steady presence at the helm, or the ability to weather leadership changes smoothly, can ensure the long-term vision is not lost.

Flexibility and Adaptability

The context and system surrounding a CI partnership are continually changing, therefore flexibility and adaptability are important promoters of sustainability. Blythe Butler is the Acting Network Weaver for the First 2000 Days Network, a CI initiative for early childhood development in Calgary, Alberta. When it comes to sustaining their network she says, *"Complex-adaptive challenges require complex-adaptive solutions. The extent to which we can match our solution design to the changing dynamics of the system over time determines our ability to sustain positive change in the long run."*

Seek a Critical Mass

Sustaining CI momentum is easier when everyone comes to the party. In the Rio Grande Valley in Texas, over forty organizations representing the vast majority of students in the region are involved in a CI initiative to improve academic outcomes. Leaders from K-12 and post-secondary institutions, community-based agencies, workforce organizations, and philanthropy groups come together regularly to develop and monitor CI strategies. Wynn Rosser at the Greater Texas Foundation believes this critical mass of participants has a positive influence on their sustainability because it makes it easier to challenge the system and work towards transformative change when almost everyone is involved. In his words, *"There is more political safety for doing something very different, even daring, because they are working as a group. There is typically safety in the average, doing what everyone else does, and what everyone else does is usually the status quo. In the Rio*

cont'd

Grande Valley, though, what everyone else does is systemic transformation. Leaders want to be a part of it."[11]

The Personal Factor

Sometimes the motivation to continue comes simply from the personalities around the table. As Fay Hanleybrown, John Kania, and Mark Kramer say, "...*perhaps the most important sustaining factor for change is a connection to one another at the most human of levels, the place where personal purpose comes together with shared purpose."[12]* Creating social opportunities for members to get to know and enjoy each other's company can help reinforce their commitment over time.

[11] Rosser, W. (2016, February 17). Sustaining momentum in collective impact: A story from the Rio Grande Valley of Texas. Retrieved from http://collectiveimpact hforum.org/blogs/1521/sustaining-momentumcollective-impact---story-rio-grande-valley-texas.

[12] Hanleybrown, F., Kania, J., & Kramer, M. (2012, January 26). Channeling change: Making collective impact work. Stanford Social Innovation Review. Retrieved from http://ssir.org/articles/entry/channeling_change_making_collective_impact_work.

Program Champions

Another very significant promoter of sustainability is a program champion. These individuals are well-positioned advocates of your program who use their connections, influence, prestige, and charisma to carry out a number of important functions including:

- providing a vision
- mobilizing people and resources
- creating strategic linkages among diverse stakeholders
- generating different types of support
- channeling resources
- obtaining publicity
- influencing policy change

Program champions may be internal or external to your program. However, they are usually not staff. The power of a champion comes from their voluntary connection to your program. While your manager or executive director might be an extremely strong and effective leader, the type of champion I'm referring to is a busy, respected, and external individual who has chosen your program above others as the one they wish to support. For nonprofits and charities, these are often recognized leaders from the community, local business, school board, or local government. They may be on your board, or they may not. In large institutions, they are often senior executives or upper-level managers who are in your corner when you need them. Sometimes a champion is the original visionary or founder of a program who still maintains a helpful connection. In other cases, they might be a previous client or beneficiary who can speak with conviction on how effective and reputable your services are. Champions even exist in government in the form of elected representatives or public servants who can help you source funding or negotiate government bureaucracy. Wherever they come from, they usually have a combination of the following personal qualities:

- passionate about your issue
- strong commitment
- excellent interpersonal skills
- good negotiation skills

- strong leadership skills
- good at recruiting and motivating people

Champions play such a pivotal role in building program sustainability that I've devoted a whole chapter to them in Chapter 11, including a special Champions Identification Worksheet to help you source and recruit them.

Personnel

Strong & Continuous Leadership

Sustainable programs tend to be headed by strong and competent organizational leaders who are committed to seeing the program's long-term goals come to fruition. But it's not just about having a competent senior manager; it also helps to have continuity in these key leadership positions over time. Sometimes the general public perceives high management turnover as an indication of deeper organization dysfunction. This perception can discourage external partners, funders, champions, and stakeholders from providing support. This can also apply to other forms of leadership such as your board of directors or advisory boards.

Local Program Staff

Programs that employ local residents as program staff are associated with greater sustainability. This is likely related to the staff's ability to better reflect local values and culture and foster greater community buy-in and ownership.

Champions play a pivotal role in building program sustainability.

Engaged Funders

Sustainability research has also found a relationship between programs with higher than normal funder involvement and long-term sustainability. Consider the relationship that you have with your funder(s). In many cases, you may just be a name and program description on a grant application form. However, funders who are familiar with you and your program will have a better understanding and appreciation of your issue area. They have seen the services you provide in action and have possibly talked first hand to some of your participants, making them more likely to advocate for renewal of your funding when the time comes. The challenge for you is to distinguish yourself and your program in their minds in a way that changes your program from simply a name on a grant application form to real people, effectively working for real change. This does not mean simply emailing them your monthly newsletter. You might consider approaching them for their valued opinion on a current sector-wide issue, or inviting them to an open house. If you can address confidentiality issues appropriately, consider inviting funders for a site visit that allows them to observe the program in action. Create opportunities for them to visit via small celebrations such as a program graduation. Or ask them to join your board for a social lunch and learn. Give them a reason to have an interesting conversation with you over the phone or a compelling excuse to get out of the office and meet your amazing staff and clients first hand.

Host Agency

Fit with Host Agency

In Chapter 1, we looked at the different types of sustainability and mentioned how one type involves the transition of a program from pilot status into a more stable core program by its host or backbone agency. A host agency is to a pilot what a greenhouse is to a seedling. It provides a temporary home and acts as a fiscal agent until the pilot either transforms into a core program within that agency or finds a new home with another organization. This process is called "institutionalization" and occurs when the host agency considers the pilot's benefits to outweigh the costs and progressively absorbs it into the larger agency budget.

A host agency is to a pilot what a greenhouse is to a seedling.

Not4Profit @Not4Profit

Office space available for rent in renovated 1850s mansion in Baltimore's Mt. Vernon community. If interested or know others who might be let us know @not4profit

However, for this to occur, there must be a good "fit" between the host agency and the program. The problem area, program goals, organizational mission, current strategic priorities, and program/organizational culture must match. Consider the previous analogy of your pilot project as a seedling. While some greenhouses will provide the right conditions for growth, others will not. Many established organizations are in a position to provide desk space and other forms of support to new pilot initiatives, but might not be invested in their overall success. Research tells us that the uptake of a pilot to a more stable home is more likely to occur if there is some alignment between the mandate of the pilot and the mission of the host agency. For example, the chances are that a water conservation initiative will not flourish as well with a literacy organization as it would with a botanical society. If you are looking for a host agency for your pilot, pay attention to fit and choose wisely because it's hard to change later.

Host Agency Capacity

The more mature the host agency, the better their capacity to support and nurture a pilot towards sustainability. Larger, stable organizations with good reputations are often able to leverage resources when necessary and provide things like financial buffers, logistical support, communications and fundraising assistance, and leadership guidance.

Community

Strong Community Support

Community support plays a significant role in promoting program sustainability. The involvement of community members increases their ownership and long-term commitment to your program, which in turn enhances long-term sustainability. Early organizational development consultant, Richard Beckhard, noted it best when he said, "People support what they helped create."[13] But what do we mean by "support"? Community support is a concept that receives a lot of lip service in our field but little action on the ground. I like to think of a program with strong and diverse community support as having stakeholders who are highly receptive to the issue and its significance, along with active (not token) community participation in program planning, implementation, and evaluation.

People support what they helped create.
~ Richard Beckhard

---

[13]Beckhard, R. (1969). Organization development: strategies and models. Reading, MA.: Addison-Wesley. p. 114.

As a key manager or staff person, you are the one who knows best where and how to achieve this involvement. A good place to start is determining, *"Who loves us, needs us, and would care if we were gone?"*[14] Once you know who these supporters are, you can begin to cultivate them into a constituency that is ready and waiting to rally to save your program if it is threatened. But this cultivation takes time and is not a quick fix for a struggling program.

Local Government, Policy Maker, and Business Support

Sustainability researchers have also found that there is a relationship between support from other entities such as local government, policy makers, and business, and your program's sustainability. This support might take the form of unofficial backing from your city council, or material donations from local businesses. Whatever it is, it can bolster your sustainability by increasing your credibility, diversifying your revenue, and positioning you publicly as a valued community resource.

Communications

High Visibility

I'm sure you're aware of many excellent programs that are making positive impacts in your community. But does everyone know this? There is a lot of noise in our everyday lives, and it's easy for your program to get lost amidst competing voices. At the same time, busy program managers usually have their heads down working diligently on day-to-day issues and neglect to pop their heads up once in a while to tell the world what they've achieved. Unfortunately, communications is an activity that frequently gets dropped off the table, to the detriment of not only your public profile but also your sustainability. How can people support you if they don't know who you are, what you do, and what you've accomplished?

Strategic Communications

Enter strategic communications. A formal communications plan can go a long way towards building the support you need to thrive. What messages will resonate with your different stakeholders to gain and keep their attention? Programs with a clear communications plan are better able to pro-

[14] The Finance Project. (2002). Sustaining comprehensive community initiatives: Key elements for success. Washington, DC: The Finance Project. Retrieved from http://www.financeprojectinfo.org/Publications/Sustaining.pdf.

mote their successes and develop a constituency of support in their community. Since this is not always a skill of program staff, you may need to seek special funds to pay for this, or find a knowledge philanthropist willing to provide pro bono services.

Look Familiar?

Do any of these factors seem familiar? I'm guessing that you're probably acquainted with many of them already. As I often say in my workshops, sustainability is not rocket science. In fact, if I had to describe these factors I would say that most of them are recognized best practices for operating a program or nonprofit. In fact, the longer a program is in existence, the greater its potential for long-term sustainability. One of the reasons for this is that it has had more time to demonstrate positive outcomes, increase its credibility among stakeholders, develop a community profile, and grow a larger base of support, which are all in themselves promoters of sustainability.

When you look at these factors, I think you'll also agree that increasing your sustainability is not just about applying for more grants. I've just given you twenty-eight areas where you can intervene in more concrete and practical ways.

Now that you know what factors are associated with program sustainability, I'll explain how you can begin to plan for sustainability. In the following chapter, I'll introduce you to a straightforward three-step system for developing your own sustainability plan.

It's Not Just About Resources

Guelph-Wellington Local Immigration Partnership

Staff and volunteers at the Guelph-Wellington Local Immigration Partnership (LIP) knew they needed to deal with the sustainability of their new initiative sooner rather than later, but they often struggled with what that actually meant. They knew they had two years of funding but no idea of what would happen after that. They also realized that having only one funder made them vulnerable. After taking my webinar on sustainability planning, they had a better idea of what they needed to do. Volunteer Geetha Van den Daele says, *"In the beginning, it was a challenge to talk about, but having a better understanding of the 28 factors of sustainability has helped us to have a more productive conversation with our partners about addressing it."* Building in more opportunities for grassroots volunteers, recruiting program champions, carrying out a comprehensive evaluation, and raising their community profile are just some of the areas in which they've lately focused their efforts. Alex Goss, LIP project manager, notes, *"Now we understand it's not just about resources, there's a whole range of other factors to consider."* They've also managed to transfer two of their early initiatives, a mentoring program, and a volunteer bank, to more secure homes at other host organizations. Although they are not one hundred percent sustainable at this point, Goss does feel they are starting to see the benefits of adopting a sustainability perspective. *"Staff are beginning to think about our continuation options,"* he says, *"and that's good."* Their advice for other organizations embarking on sustainability planning is to understand it and consider it sooner. As Goss says, *"Knowing the factors of sustainability earlier on would have been helpful. If we'd had a better understanding of them, we'd probably be a year ahead of where we are at this point."* However, Van den Daele also notes that *"It does take time, though. We couldn't have built a plan right away. Our partnership needed first to work out what our new role was and how we were going to work together. We weren't ready at the beginning, but now it's hitting home, and there's more buy-in and understanding from our members on sustainability."* Guelph-Wellington LIP has now formed a dedicated sustainability team that is developing a plan that involves all partners around the table. One of their first steps has been to assess their organization's sustainability using the Program Sustainability Assessment Tool (see Chapter 5), which they plan to do annually.

Chapter 3
SUMMARY

- Research in the field of program sustainability is relatively new but provides insights into what factors are associated with increased program longevity.

- There are 28 factors related to program sustainability that appear regularly in research studies. These factors fall into the areas of external funding, planning and evaluation, program design, partners, personnel, host agency, community, and communications. Awareness of these factors is the first step towards developing effective sustainability strategies.

- Some of the strongest promoters of program sustainability are diversified revenue, a program evaluation, collaborative partnerships, community support, a program champion(s), and a sustainability plan.

Learning Objectives

In this chapter, you will learn:

- Three steps in planning for program sustainability.
- The best time to begin sustainability planning.
- Four tips for facilitating the sustainability planning process.

Chapter 4: The Sustainability Planning Process

Three Steps to Increasing Your Sustainability

In Chapters 1 through 3, we looked at what program sustainability is, why it's important, and what factors promote it. Over the next seven chapters, I will introduce you to a three-step process to develop a sustainability plan.

Step 1 - Assess *(Chapters 5 - 6)*

- Diagnose your current sustainability capacity
- Identify areas for developing sustainability strategies
- Clarify your sustainability goals

Step 2 – Plan *(Chapters 7 – 11)*

- Pinpoint future periods of potential funding instability
- Prioritize which parts of your program you would save if funding was significantly cut or reduced
- Specify concrete sustainability strategies

Step 3 - Implement *(Chapter 12)*

- Draft an action plan to facilitate follow-through

When Should I Start Thinking About Sustainability?

The simple answer to this question is NOW. Not three months before your funding ends, not when you wake up in the middle of the night worrying, and certainly not when you get a sudden notice that your funding will be cut. Building capacity to sustain your program will take time and effort, so the sooner you start, the better.

Although your program might have been around for years, it's never too late to start planning for your sustainability. If you're trying to fund a new pilot, ideally you will have already included sustainability planning into your initial program plans so you can readily answer questions about it on grant application forms.

How Do I Plan for Sustainability?

If you stick to the three step process I've outlined above, you'll have an effective and structured path to follow. Here are some additional tips to facilitate your efforts.

Tips

Don't Do it Alone

Sustainability planning is not something you do off the side of your desk. It's a large-scale brainstorming and consensus-building activity. It's somewhat similar to strategic planning or risk planning in that your sustainability strategies emerge from thoughtful consideration of your existing assets and where you need to improve. In fact, your sustainability plan can often drive your next strategic plan. But you would never develop a strategic plan on your own, and neither should you do your sustainability plan alone. Sustainability planning is an activity best done by a group of your staff and any other stakeholders you think might add to the conversation. Some sustainability strategies can be far reaching, so make sure you have a good mix of participants who are familiar with the program and have the power to implement the plan. Leadership buy-in and support is particularly important. Inviting existing partners is also highly recommended. This is also a good time to include any program champions and knowledgeable community members to begin building the constituency of support I discussed in Chapter 3. You might even choose to convene a temporary Sustainability Working Group. Here's some good news: sustainability planning is actually fun. I've facilitated dozens of sustainability planning

cont'd

sessions over the years, and participants tell me they enjoy the opportunity to reflect on their program in a positive and purposeful way. They find it validating to identify other entities who share their desire to succeed, as well as brainstorm concrete steps forward. They leave feeling energized and full of solutions rather than dragged down with a bunch of problems.

Create the Time and Space
Many organizations choose to develop their strategic plans during a retreat, and it's the same for sustainability planning. Getting staff away from their day-to-day responsibilities and pressures can open up their minds to focus on creative ways to pursue greater sustainability.

Allocate Time, But Not Too Much
Here's some more good news. Unlike some planning processes, you can complete your sustainability planning relatively quickly. It has a beginning and an end and shouldn't drag on and on. In my experience, most groups can accomplish about eighty percent of their sustainability plan in a single day-long session. All that remains is to put the finishing touches on a follow-through action plan, which, in my opinion, should never be done at the end of a long day when people are tired.

Get Help if Needed
If you're a skilled meeting chair and comfortable facilitating large group brainstorming and building consensus among your staff, you'll be able to run your sustainability planning session easily. If you're not, arrange for a professional facilitator to help you. Any consultant or knowledge philanthropist familiar with strategic planning will be able to facilitate this process comfortably once you give them this book and the three steps. One benefit of using an outside facilitator is that you'll be able to participate in the process yourself.

Session One

9:00 - 9:20	**Welcome and Introductions** • Agenda and objectives for the day • Housekeeping items
9:20 - 10:30	**Introduction to Sustainability** • What it is • Why it's important • Factors influencing program sustainability
10:30 - 10:45	*Break*
10:45 - 11:30	**Step 1 - Assess** • Program Sustainability Assessment Tool
11:30 - 12:00	**Step 2 - Plan** • The Funding Matrix
12:00 - 1:00	*Lunch*
1:00 - 2:30	**Step 2 - Plan (continued)** • Worst Case Scenario • Systems Map
2:30 - 2:45	*Break*
2:45 - 3:50	**Step 2 - Plan (continued)** • Strategizing for Sustainability • Identifying Program Champions
3:50 - 4:00	**Wrap-up and Next Steps**

Session Two

9:00 - 9:20	**Review of Session One work**
9:20 - 10:30	**Step 3 - Implement** • Sustainability Action Plan
10:30 - 10:45	*Break*
10:45 - 11:30	**Step 3 - Implement** • Sustainability Action Plan (continued)
11:30 - 12:00	Wrap-up and Next Steps

Note that Session Two can occur at any point after the main planning session. Many organizations choose to convene a smaller working group for this portion of the sustainability planning process. At this point, the work of the first session has been typed up for review during the second session.

Sample Sustainability Planning Agenda

Two Cautionary Notes

Although sustainability planning is relatively easy, I do have two cautionary notes for you:

1. There are no magic bullets to solve your sustainability woes.

As we've seen in Chapter 3, sustainability is a complex issue dependent on a whole host of factors. If I could wave my magic wand and send you ten more years of core funding, believe me, I would. But sustainability doesn't come that easily. However, achieving sustainability is possible, because many organizations before you have done it. Those who are willing to think creatively, roll up their sleeves, and get to work on several strategies at once will be rewarded over the long term.

2. Finding the time to implement your sustainability strategies can be a challenge.

In previous roles, I have been a busy program manager and I fully understand the challenges you face continually, trying to squeeze too much into an already over-packed day. The result of your sustainability planning process will indeed produce strategies that will require additional time and effort on your part to implement. In Chapter 12 I will give you some tips to help keep your implementation on track.

In Chapters 7 through 12, I'm going to show you specific activities to help you develop your sustainability plan. But first you need to determine your existing sustainability strengths and weaknesses, which we'll do in the next chapter.

Chapter 4
SUMMARY

- The three steps in sustainability planning are Assess, Plan, and Implement.

- The best time to begin sustainability planning is immediately. Building capacity to sustain your program will take time and effort, so the sooner you start, the better.

- Whether your program is new or old, it's never too late to start planning for your sustainability.

- Four tips for facilitating the sustainability planning process are: don't do it alone, create appropriate time and space (such as a stakeholder retreat), don't let it drag on, and get facilitation help if needed.

Step I - Assess

To begin your sustainability planning, you need to have a good grasp of your program's existing strengths and weaknesses from a sustainability perspective. Once you know your capacity in this area, you can effectively prioritize areas for attention. This next section will introduce you to a useful online tool that will assess your program's current sustainability in several key dimensions.

Learning Objectives

In this chapter, you will learn:

- How to use the Program Sustainability Assessment Tool.

Chapter 5: The Program Sustainability Assessment Tool

There are several tools out there to help you assess your program's level of sustainability, but the one I like the best is the web-based Program Sustainability Tool (PSAT) available on page 73 and at *www.sustaintool.org*.[15] Developed by the Center for Public Health Systems Science at Washington University in St. Louis, the PSAT allows you to rate your programs on several dimensions that research has shown increase your likelihood of sustainability. Although the Center originally developed it for chronic disease prevention programs, I believe it's relevant for most types of programs. The tool is quick, user-friendly, and best of all gives you a score that you can use to evaluate the success of your efforts over time. You can complete the assessment individually or as a large group. Two options for group administration are to have participants complete it before the retreat and bring their answers to discuss in a large group, or complete it together as a group. If you complete it online, the tool will automatically generate a graph displaying your current sustainability capacity by domain, similar to the example below.

Sustainability Capacity by Domain

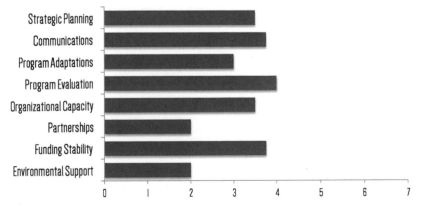

[15] Luke, D.A., Calhoun, A., Robichaux, C.B., Elliott, M.B., Moreland-Russell, S. (2014). The program sustainability assessment tool: A new instrument for public health programs. Preventing Chronic Disease, 11, 130184. Used with permission.

Either way, I find the biggest benefit is the debriefing that follows. First of all, the tool gives you a baseline score that you can use to gauge your progress over time. Secondly, many groups find it validates their previous accomplishments in certain areas. However, the tool's developers are quick to point out that a high score in any one domain does not necessarily guarantee a level of sustainability. In my sessions, I find it's an excellent way to kick-start the group discussion, get everyone thinking about their current sustainability capacity, and begin the process of brainstorming and prioritizing sustainability strategies. These initial strategies will come in handy when you move on to Step 2 - Plan.

Identifying Sustainability Strengths and Weaknesses

Gibsons Landing Fibre Arts Festival

The board and staff of the Gibsons Landing Fibre Arts Festival began their day-long sustainability planning session by individually assessing their current sustainability capacity. A large group debrief yielded the following insights.

Our Sustainability Strengths

Program evaluation
- We conduct a process evaluation every year after our event to see how we can improve operations and delivery.

Organizational Capacity
- We are lean and operate on a core group of skilled volunteers.

Funding Stability
- Our funding is relatively diversified for an organization of our size.

Environmental Support
- Data from a recent Regional Cultural Scan emphasizes the need for our event.
- We have good support from the community, local government, and businesses.

Areas to Work On

Communications
- Increase our visibility locally and provincially.
- Better highlight what is unique about our festival.
- Promote our successes and positive economic impacts more widely.

Program Evaluation
- Conduct an outcome evaluation every few years to determine what positive impacts the festival brings to the community and local business.

Organizational Capacity
- Increase our internal capacity to deal with volunteer burnout.
- Source funds to hire a part-time staff person.

Partnerships
- Build more partnerships with other destination marketing organizations in our region.

Funding Stability
- Expand our number of festival sponsors.
- Expand earned income opportunities during the festival and throughout the year.
- Diversify our grant sources.

Environmental Support
- Make formal community presentations to municipal leaders, service organizations, and other groups.

These insights were recorded on a flipchart and formed the basis of many of their later sustainability strategies.

Try It!

Name: Program Sustainability Assessment Tool
Purpose: To assess the sustainability of new or ongoing programs.
Materials: none

Steps:

1. Instruct all participants to complete the tool either individually (before, or during the session), in small groups, or as a large group. If it is a large group, consider projecting it onto a large screen.

2. Determine each overall average score and average domain scores. One option to make things more interactive is to have everyone plot their scores for each domain on a radar chart using a piece of flip chart similar to the following example. Draw a spider web with eight axes. Label each axis with one of the eight PSAT domains. Starting from the centre, number the top vertical axis one through seven. Ask participants to place or draw a dot with their score on the axis of each corresponding domain. You will be able to see the amount of agreement or disagreement in the group by how closely the dots cluster.

3. Debrief the results by posing questions to the large group such as:

   - Which areas are present to a large extent? Why?
   - Which areas are present to a lesser extent? Why?
   - What appear to be our sustainability strengths and weaknesses?
   - Where do we agree and disagree on the results?
   - Do any of these results surprise you? Why?
   - Which domains are a priority for us to address?
   - Which are the most amenable to change?
   - Which areas would give us the biggest bang for our buck in terms of effort?

4. Record the group's ideas on two flip charts, one with the heading "Sustainability Strengths" and one with "Sustainability Weaknesses". Post these in a central area where people can refer to them during later activities.

5. To monitor your progress, it's a great idea to complete the assessment again one year later. You can plot before and after scores on your radar chart like the following example. The area in blue represents your initial scores and the area in red shows how you may have grown in each dimension over time.

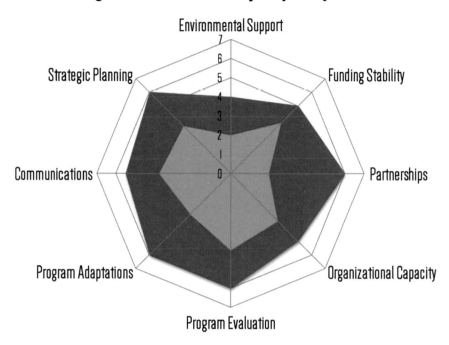

Changes in Sustainability Capacity Over Time

Congratulations! By assessing your program, you've taken the first step in developing a sustainability plan for your program. In the next chapter let's look at setting some sustainability goals.

Program Sustainability Assessment Tool

What is program sustainability capacity?

We define program sustainability capacity as *the ability to maintain programming and its benefits over time.*

Why is program sustainability capacity important?

Programs at all levels and settings struggle with their sustainability capacity. Unfortunately, when programs are forced to shut down, hard won improvements in public health, clinical care, or social service outcomes can dissolve. To maintain these benefits to society, stakeholders must understand all of the factors that contribute to program sustainability. With knowledge of these critical factors, stakeholders can build program *capacity* for sustainability and position their efforts for long term success.

What is the purpose of this tool?

This tool will enable you to assess your program's current capacity for sustainability across a range of specific organizational and contextual factors. Your responses will identify sustainability strengths and challenges. You can then use results to guide sustainability action planning for your program.

Helpful definitions

This tool has been designed for use with a wide variety of programs, both large and small, across different settings. Given this flexibility, it is important for you to think through how you are defining your program, organization, and community before starting the assessment.

Below are a few definitions of terms that are frequently used throughout the tool.

- **Program** refers to the set of formal organized activities that you want to sustain over time. Such activities could occur at the local, state, national, or international level and in a variety of settings.
- **Organization** encompasses all the parent organizations or agencies in which the program is housed. Depending on your program, the organization may refer to a national, state, or local department, a nonprofit organization, a hospital, etc.
- **Community** refers to the stakeholders who may benefit from or who may guide the program. This could include local residents, organizational leaders, decision-makers, etc. Community does not refer to a specific town or neighborhood.

Center for Public Health Systems Science

GEORGE WARREN BROWN SCHOOL OF SOCIAL WORK

The name of the program or set of activities I am assessing is:

_____

In the following questions, you will rate your program across a range of specific factors that affect sustainability. Please respond to as many items as possible. If you truly feel you are not able to answer an item, you may select "NA." **For each statement, circle the number that best indicates the extent to which your program has or does the following things.**

Political Support: Internal and external political environments that support your program

	To little or no extent					To a very great extent		Not able to answer
1. Political champions advocate for the program.	1	2	3	4	5	6	7	NA
2. The program has strong champions with the ability to garner resources.	1	2	3	4	5	6	7	NA
3. The program has political support within the larger organization.	1	2	3	4	5	6	7	NA
4. The program has political support from outside of the organization.	1	2	3	4	5	6	7	NA
5. The program has strong advocacy support.	1	2	3	4	5	6	7	NA

Funding Stability: Establishing a consistent financial base for your program

	To little or no extent					To a very great extent		Not able to answer
1. The program exists in a supportive state economic climate.	1	2	3	4	5	6	7	NA
2. The program implements policies to help ensure sustained funding.	1	2	3	4	5	6	7	NA
3. The program is funded through a variety of sources.	1	2	3	4	5	6	7	NA
4. The program has a combination of stable and flexible funding.	1	2	3	4	5	6	7	NA
5. The program has sustained funding.	1	2	3	4	5	6	7	NA

For each statement, circle the number that best indicates the extent to which your program has or does the following things.

Partnerships: Cultivating connections between your program and its stakeholders

	To little or no extent					To a very great extent		Not able to answer
1. Diverse community organizations are invested in the success of the program.	1	2	3	4	5	6	7	NA
2. The program communicates with community leaders.	1	2	3	4	5	6	7	NA
3. Community leaders are involved with the program.	1	2	3	4	5	6	7	NA
4. Community members are passionately committed to the program.	1	2	3	4	5	6	7	NA
5. The community is engaged in the development of program goals.	1	2	3	4	5	6	7	NA

Organizational Capacity: Having the internal support and resources needed to effectively manage your program and its activities

	To little or no extent					To a very great extent		Not able to answer
1. The program is well integrated into the operations of the organization.	1	2	3	4	5	6	7	NA
2. Organizational systems are in place to support the various program needs.	1	2	3	4	5	6	7	NA
3. Leadership effectively articulates the vision of the program to external partners.	1	2	3	4	5	6	7	NA
4. Leadership efficiently manages staff and other resources.	1	2	3	4	5	6	7	NA
5. The program has adequate staff to complete the program's goals.	1	2	3	4	5	6	7	NA

For each statement, circle the number that best indicates the extent to which your program has or does the following things.

Program Evaluation: Assessing your program to inform planning and document results

	To little or no extent					To a very great extent		Not able to answer
1. The program has the capacity for quality program evaluation.	1	2	3	4	5	6	7	NA
2. The program reports short term and intermediate outcomes.	1	2	3	4	5	6	7	NA
3. Evaluation results inform program planning and implementation.	1	2	3	4	5	6	7	NA
4. Program evaluation results are used to demonstrate successes to funders and other key stakeholders.	1	2	3	4	5	6	7	NA
5. The program provides strong evidence to the public that the program works.	1	2	3	4	5	6	7	NA

Program Adaptation: Taking actions that adapt your program to ensure its ongoing effectiveness

	To little or no extent					To a very great extent		Not able to answer
1. The program periodically reviews the evidence base.	1	2	3	4	5	6	7	NA
2. The program adapts strategies as needed.	1	2	3	4	5	6	7	NA
3. The program adapts to new science.	1	2	3	4	5	6	7	NA
4. The program proactively adapts to changes in the environment.	1	2	3	4	5	6	7	NA
5. The program makes decisions about which components are ineffective and should not continue.	1	2	3	4	5	6	7	NA

For each statement, circle the number that best indicates the extent to which your program has or does the following things.

Communications: Strategic communication with stakeholders and the public about your program

	To little or no extent					To a very great extent		Not able to answer
1. The program has communication strategies to secure and maintain public support.	1	2	3	4	5	6	7	NA
2. Program staff communicate the need for the program to the public.	1	2	3	4	5	6	7	NA
3. The program is marketed in a way that generates interest.	1	2	3	4	5	6	7	NA
4. The program increases community awareness of the issue.	1	2	3	4	5	6	7	NA
5. The program demonstrates its value to the public.	1	2	3	4	5	6	7	NA

Strategic Planning: Using processes that guide your program's direction, goals, and strategies

	To little or no extent					To a very great extent		Not able to answer
1. The program plans for future resource needs.	1	2	3	4	5	6	7	NA
2. The program has a long-term financial plan.	1	2	3	4	5	6	7	NA
3. The program has a sustainability plan.	1	2	3	4	5	6	7	NA
4. The program's goals are understood by all stakeholders.	1	2	3	4	5	6	7	NA
5. The program clearly outlines roles and responsibilities for all stakeholders.	1	2	3	4	5	6	7	NA

Program Sustainability Assessment Tool

Rating Instructions

Once you have completed the Program Sustainability Assessment Tool, transfer your responses to this rating sheet to calculate your average scores. Please record the score for each item (1-7), or write "NA" if you were not able to answer.

		Political Support	Funding Stability	Partnerships	Organizational Capacity	Program Evaluation	Program Adaptation	Communications	Strategic Planning
ITEM	1.								
	2.								
	3.								
	4.								
	5.								

DOMAIN

Domain Total: Add up your scores in each column. Exclude 'NA'

Average Score for Domain: Divide the domain total by the total number of items with a score. Exclude 'NA'

Overall Score: Average together all the domain scores

Use these results to guide sustainability action planning for your program. The domains with lower average scores indicate areas where your program's capacity for sustainability could be improved.

Center for Public Health Systems Science

GEORGE WARREN BROWN
SCHOOL OF SOCIAL WORK

Chapter 5
SUMMARY

- The Program Sustainability Assessment Tool is an easy way to assess your program's current state of sustainability.

- The tool provides a baseline score for monitoring your sustainability efforts over time, facilitates group discussion regarding your current strengths and challenges, and begins to prioritize areas requiring a sustainability strategy.

Learning Objectives

In this chapter, you will learn:

- To set your own sustainability goals.

Chapter 6: How Do You Know You've Achieved Sustainability?

In Chapter 1, I talked about the various types of sustainability to strive for. Because there are different kinds, what it looks like for you will depend on the particular type and context of your program. For some of you, it will simply be functioning at your original capacity through the addition of more diversified revenue, new partners, and possibly new program champions. For others, it might mean finding a better-suited host or backbone agency, or transitioning into a core program. Other markers of sustainability might include:

- the continuation of certain parts of your program as it evolves and adapts
- the integration of new practices, procedures, and policies into daily operations
- the maintenance of benefits for your clients that render the service unnecessary
- scaling up in size or to other sites.

What are your sustainability goals? Where is your program on the Continuum of Sustainability? What is reasonable to expect for a program of your type, size, age, or design? Remember that total self-sufficiency is a difficult and likely impossible goal for most programs, so be realistic about what you can achieve.

Sustainability is an orientation, not a destination. Sometimes the phrase "sustainable business model" sounds as if it refers to a place that, once reached, will allow the organization to generate financial resources on an ongoing basis while the board and staff sit back, relax, and watch it happen. But what is sustainable today may be unsustainable tomorrow. Funding streams dry up or shift focus; programmatic practices evolve; client populations change. We never arrive at a mix of programs and revenue streams that can be described as permanently sustainable. But we can always be heading in the right direction.[16]

[16] Bell, J., Masaoka, J. & Zimmerman, S. (2010). Nonprofit sustainability: Making strategic decisions for financial viability (p. 13). San Francisco, CA: Jossey-Bass.

You will likely always be working on some aspect of your sustainability, with some program elements partially sustained and others not. But having some clear goals prior to embarking on your sustainability plan will help you develop coherent strategies.

In this chapter, we looked at the importance of setting clear sustainability goals. In the next few chapters, we'll look at several activities you can do with your group to elicit more concrete steps for enhancing your sustainability.

Chapter 6
SUMMARY

- Your sustainability goals will depend on the particular type and context of your program. Different programs will aim for different locations on the Continuum of Sustainability.

- Complete self-sufficiency is a difficult and largely impossible goal for most programs. Be realistic about what you can achieve.

- Having clear sustainability goals will help you develop appropriate sustainability strategies.

Step 2 - Plan

Over the next few chapters I'm going to introduce you to five more incredibly useful exercises to use during your sustainability planning session:

- The Funding Matrix
- Worst Case Scenario
- Finding New Support
- Strategizing for Sustainability
- Identifying Program Champions

Individually, each of these exercises will give you a unique perspective on your program's sustainability. Together, they will build a solid foundation for your sustainability plan.

Learning Objectives

In this chapter, you will learn about:

- Identifying future periods of possible funding insecurity.

Chapter 7: The Funding Matrix

I f I asked you how many sources of funding your program has, you might be able to tell me immediately. For some of you, however, it could be more challenging. These days it's common for programs to have more than one or two funding bodies. In my workshops, I regularly have participants tell me they juggle six, seven, and even eight grants for one program. While this is a good thing in terms of diversity of revenue, it can get confusing when these sources of funding don't begin and end at the same time. The more sources of revenue, the greater the complexity of managing it.

The Funding Matrix below can be a big help in these situations. Originally developed by the Center for Civic Partnerships for their *Sustainability Toolkit*,[17] it illustrates at a glance both the current and future funding outlook of your program. It can alert you to:

- when significant funding will end
- upcoming windows of opportunity for applying for new funding
- ways that funding can be reallocated within the program
- opportunities to expand current funding sources
- possible new sources

Take a look at the example on the next page of a fictitious Family Resource Centre. Listed across the top are their different funding sources along with the time remaining and whether or not there is an option to renew. Down the left-hand side is a breakdown of all the different elements of the program, from administration to individual services.

[17] Center for Civic Partnerships. (2011). 10 steps to maintaining your community improvements, 2nd edition. Sacramento, CA: Public Health Institute. Available from http://www.civicpartnerships.org.

Funding Matrix Worksheet – Family Resource Centre

Funding Sources	Good Works Foundation	Ministry of Caring	Regional Gaming Commission	Federal Department of Happiness	Collaborative Partners	Other Community Sources (businesses, volunteers)	Total Cash	Total In-Kind
Funding Ends	[date]	[date]	[date]	[date]	[date]	?		
Time Remaining	21 months	8 months	11 months	9 months	21 months	?		
Option to Renew?	no	don't know	yes	don't know	yes	yes		
Funding Applied to:								
Administration (personnel, etc.)		$25,000		$10,000			$35,000	
Parent & Tot Drop-in			$30,000	$20,000		$1,000	$51,000	
Toy Library	$5,000				$2,000 (in-kind)[18]		$5,000	$2,000
Childminding		$5,000	$3,000				$8,000	
Parenting Workshop Series					$5,000	$500 (in-kind)[19]	$5,000	$500
Mother Goose Early Literacy	$15,000				$1,000 (in-kind)[20]		$15,000	$1,000
Total Cash	$20,000	$30,000	$33,000	$30,000	$5,000	$1,000	$119,000	
Total In-Kind					$3,000	$500		$3,500

[18] Space donated by the local church.
[19] Donated advertising space.
[20] Space donated by the local library.

Center for Civic Partnerships. (2011). Sustainability toolkit: 10 steps to maintaining your community improvements, 2nd edition. Sacramento, CA: Public Health Institute. Adapted with permission. Available from http://www.civicpartnerships.org.

Consider

Looking at the Funding Matrix, consider the following questions:

- Which funding sources provide the most support?
- Which funding sources provide the least?
- What do you notice about the remaining months of funding?
- What challenges does the program currently face?
- What challenges might they face in the future?
- Which funders might be able to increase their level of support?
- Who could be supporting them but isn't?
- Are there any ways that funding can be reallocated within the program?

Break it Down!

Being able to conceptualize your program not as a whole but as a group of smaller, discrete elements is an important sustainability skill. When it comes to the long-term viability of a program, many of us imagine ourselves as the Greek God Atlas, carrying the entire world, or in this case, our entire program, on our shoulders. We often believe that our program must continue exactly as is, and we struggle to find large amounts of funding to sustain the program in its entirety, rather than breaking it down into more manageable "chunks." These elements might be anything from distinct services such as outreach or different sites to other functions such as specific positions, administration, or promotion. The smaller the element, the easier it will be to find tailored solutions for that chunk from a sustainability perspective. This concept will also be important when you try the next activity in Chapter 8, the "Worst Case Scenario."

Once you have linked each funding source to the appropriate program element in the matrix and calculated individual column and row totals, you'll find it's possible to derive new and important insights about your program's funding situation.

Here are some observations we can make about our Family Resource Centre:

- They are about to lose two major sources of administrative funding in eight to nine months' time. This information is valuable as it gives the organization more lead time to start searching.

- The program receives little support from collaborative partners. Recall that collaboration is a significant promoter of sustainability as additional program partners can buffer the impacts of funding cuts.

- There is little support from business and community, both financial and in-kind.

- In-kind support is very low overall. This type of support is significantly associated with sustainability as it's sometimes easier to supplement resources through in-kind donations versus cash.

I find this exercise is particularly valuable for organizations with more than two or three funders as it visualizes their current funding scenario on

one easy to read page. When you're juggling multiple funders, it can sometimes be difficult to stay on top of end dates and reporting requirements.

Some funding bodies have fixed application cycles; analyzing the Funding Matrix can also help you align your funding requests with these cycles in a timely manner. In my sustainability planning sessions, I like to have program staff complete the matrix in advance and then give it to staff and board members to review and discuss in groups on the day of the session. Many tell me they appreciate the opportunity to view their funding situation in this manner.

You now have a tool to help you understand your current funding situation at a glance. Next, I'll show you an exercise that simulates what I call your program's "worst case scenario" and suggest how to deal with it constructively.

Try It!

Name: Funding Matrix
Purpose: To concisely display your current and future funding situation.
Materials: projector and screen

Steps:

1. Before the sustainability planning session, fill in the chart as completely as possible listing funding sources across the top and individual program elements down the side.

    -   Remember that determining new sources of funding will be easier if you break your program down into separate elements.
    -   Indicate in-kind sources separately using italics or a different colour.

2. Calculate totals for individual columns and rows.

3. Split participants into small groups and instruct them to review the matrix and consider the following questions:

    -   What challenges are we facing now? What challenges what might we face in the future?
    -   Are there any ways that we can reallocate funding within the program?
    -   Who may be able to increase their level of support?
    -   Who should be supporting us but isn't?

4. Reconvene the large group and debrief their observations. If possible, project the matrix onto a screen to facilitate discussion.

5. Record the group's observations and ideas on a flipchart for later inclusion as strategies in your sustainability plan (Chapter 10).

Tip Sometimes this isn't always as easy a process as it looks. Some programs find their funding sources don't always neatly fit into the matrix boxes. Don't be discouraged. Instead, move on to the next exercise in Chapter 8.

Chapter 7
SUMMARY

- The Funding Matrix is a tool that can visually assist you to identify upcoming periods of funding insecurity. It can also suggest ways that you can reallocate funding within your program, opportunities to expand existing revenue streams, and possible new sources.

- Being able to conceptualize your program not as a whole but as a group of smaller, discrete elements is an important sustainability skill. The smaller the element, the easier it will be to find tailored solutions for that component from a sustainability perspective.

Learning Objectives

In this chapter, you will learn:

- To prioritize what parts of your program you would save if your funding was severely cut.

Chapter 8: Worst Case Scenario

If a major funder gave you notice tomorrow that they were going to reduce your grant significantly next year, what would do? Or if you were Suzanne from Chapter 1 and your funding was being completely cut, what would you do? Although this unfortunate scenario plays out regularly for nonprofits, it's common for programs to be in denial of the very real possibility that it could happen to them. Wouldn't you rather be prepared for a situation that might never happen instead of blindsided by one you never saw coming?

The Center for Civic Partnerships has developed another great activity that I've adapted and called, "The Worst Case Scenario". At the end of this exercise, you will have a better sense of which aspects of your program you would hypothetically try to safeguard during a funding crisis, which ones you would scale back or terminate, or transfer to a more stable organization. I like to think of this activity as a way of bringing you to the edge of a scary cliff and making you peer over the edge. But in a constructive way.

This exercise is very popular with my workshop participants because it is highly visual and allows them to explore a potentially disastrous scenario in a safe, calm, and rational manner. The interactive nature of it allows for frank discussion and creative problem solving. And if done early on, it can identify and lay the groundwork for pursuing new and mutually-beneficial partnerships.

Quest for Sustainability

In the 1981 movie, Quest for Fire, a prehistoric hunter and gatherer tribe lives off the land without the knowledge of how to make fire. Because they are nomadic, they must carefully safeguard the embers of their last fire in a specially made animal hide pouch before moving on to new grazing territory. When they arrive, the first thing they must do is carefully remove the embers from the pouch, place them among small twigs, and gently blow on it until the fire returns. The Worst Case Scenario exercise is an example of this same process.

Which elements of your program are embers that you would try to safeguard until more funding came along?

What to Keep, What to Let Go?

North Okanagan Falls Prevention Program

The North Okanagan Falls Prevention Program (NOFPP) received $300,000 in federal funding over three years to conduct falls prevention workshops, peer-led home safety checks, information fairs, and a media campaign. As time moved on, and with only six months of funding left, NOFPP staff knew they were not going to receive a similar-sized grant, so they began to think seriously about their future sustainability. Some activities simply had to end, including the workshops, information fairs, and media campaign. But they were able to secure a new partnership with the regional health authority, which provided temporary funding to continue the position of part-time volunteer coordinator. The regional health authority also created a new permanent position for a Falls Prevention Manager, who began to implement the NOFPP's strategies region-wide. Some of their initiatives became institutionalized within the regional health authority's operations by providing falls prevention checklists to all health care staff. Although many of their original activities ended, their legacy continues today. The Falls Prevention Manager still works on strategies to reduce falls among seniors, and the local Seniors Information and Resource Bureau provides falls prevention information to local seniors.

Try It!

Name: Worst Case Scenario[21]

Purpose: To determine continuation options for an existing program.

Materials:
- whiteboard or blank wall space
- large sticky notes or index cards in two different colours
- markers
- masking tape

Steps:

1. Using the first set of sticky notes, instruct the group to name as many discrete activities and elements of the program as possible (see "Break it Down" pg. 87). Write each element on a sticky note. Record only one element per sticky note. Post the sticky notes as a group down the left-hand side of the whiteboard according to the example below.

Program Elements		Continuation Options				
Home Safety Checks	F/T Program Coordinator	Maintain ourselves	Scale back	Ask someone to partner or take over	Do not continue	Needs further research/ discussion
Workshops	Volunteer Coordinator					
Media Campaign	Evaluation					

2. Using a different colour of sticky note as your second set, list your Continuation Options under the scenario of a significant funding cut. These typically include:

   - Maintain Ourselves
   - Scale Back
   - Ask Someone to Partner or Take Over
   - Do Not Continue
   - Needs Further Research/Discussion

Feel free to add additional options as desired. Post these horizontally along the top of the whiteboard as column headings to the right of the first set, according to the example in Step #1.

cont'd

---

[21] Center for Civic Partnerships. (2011). Sustainability toolkit: 10 steps to maintaining your community improvements, 2nd edition. Sacramento, CA: Public Health Institute. Adapted with permission. Available from http://www.civicpartnerships.org.

Try It! cont'd

3. Instruct the group to, one at a time, place each program element sticky note on the left under one of the continuation options on the right as in the example below. Continue until all the program element sticky notes have been assigned to a continuation option column.

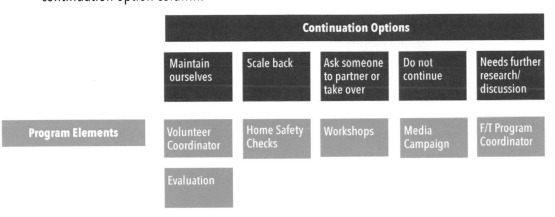

Continuation Options

Maintain ourselves	Scale back	Ask someone to partner or take over	Do not continue	Needs further research/ discussion

Program Elements

Volunteer Coordinator	Home Safety Checks	Workshops	Media Campaign	F/T Program Coordinator
Evaluation				

4. Some items will be transferred quickly, while others will generate significant discussion. Although the exercise is only hypothetical, serious trade-offs are being discussed here. Consider carefully which program activities are contributing the most to program impacts. The group may wish to reflect on program participation, satisfaction, cost, or outcomes data when making these decisions. If it's an evidence-informed program, pay attention to the minimum elements needed to achieve results.

5. If the group cannot immediately make a decision, leave it aside until all have been transferred and then retry. If the group still can't make a decision in a timely manner, place it in the final "Needs Further Research/Discussion" column.

Tip

It's common for groups to want initially to place everything in the "Maintain Ourselves" column. To avoid getting stuck, remind them that they are facing a serious (albeit hypothetical) funding shortage where it is not feasible to continue with the bulk of their current program activities. Good facilitation skills can help here.

6. Ensure that any potential partner organizations identified in the "Ask Someone to Partner or Take Over" columns are noted as you will use them again in Chapter 10. Developing these potential partnerships might be one of your future sustainability strategies.

Hopefully, you will never have to experience your worst case scenario. But if you do, you now have an exercise to help you face it head on. In the next chapter, I'll introduce you to an innovative way to use systems thinking to identify new potential stakeholders.

Chapter 8
SUMMARY

- The Worst Case Scenario is a group activity that can help you to prioritize hypothetically what components of your program you would try to safeguard if you experienced a significant drop in revenue.

- It is also useful for identifying and laying the groundwork for pursuing new partnerships that can enhance your sustainability.

Learning Objectives

In this chapter, you will learn:

- To identify new stakeholders who can support your program.

Chapter 9: Finding New Support

Remember the quote from Chapter 3 about building community support, *"Who loves you, who needs you, and who would care if you were gone?"* It is also a great concept for expanding the range of stakeholders who support the work you do. In Chapters 7 and 8, you learned about the importance of breaking your program down into more manageable chunks so that, like Atlas, you can reduce your sustainability burden. In this next exercise, you'll discover there are other like-minded people out there who might be willing to share this weight.

I've observed many programs struggling with sustainability, oblivious to the fact that there are others besides them who not only share a concern for their cause but also have a common desire to see them succeed. Discovering these new stakeholders can often open up additional avenues of support. One of the best tools for identifying these like-minded individuals and organizations is a system actor map.

A system actor map is a visual tool that illustrates the broader system that surrounds your program and the issue you are trying to address. It visualizes the relationships that influence your program as well as the complexity that surrounds it. The main benefit of a system actor map is that it depicts these relationships in a concrete way that facilitates greater insight and action. A system actor map is similar to a Mind Map[22] but with more thoughtful connections that capture what a system looks like and how it is functioning. Once you have developed your system actor map, you can explore not only the different relationships that exist between your program and other entities but also their nature and strength.

Take a look at the following examples.

---

[22] A visual depiction of information that includes a central idea surrounded by categorized branches of associated topics.

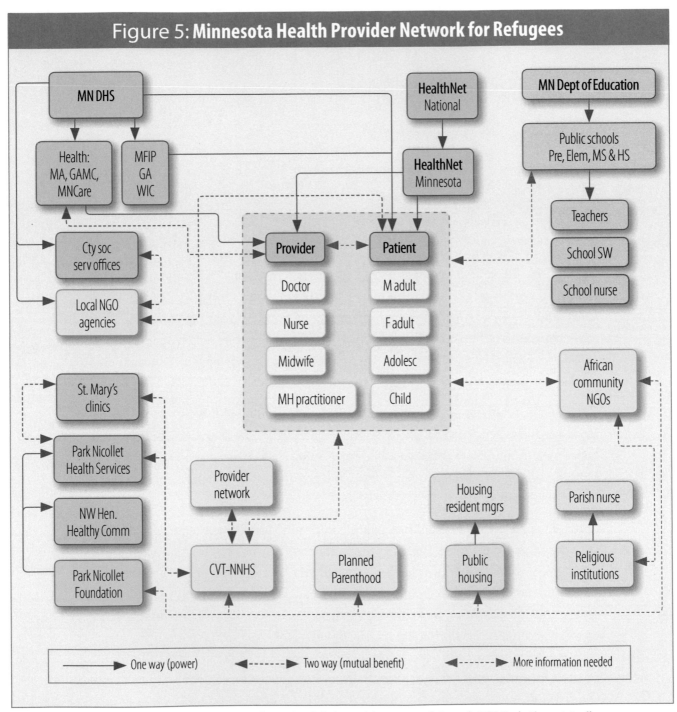

Figure 5: Minnesota Health Provider Network for Refugees

Johnson, D., & Pearson, N. (2009). Tactical mapping: How nonprofits can identify the levers of change. Nonprofit Quarterly, 16(2). Used with permission.[23]

[23] The Tactical Map tool was created initially in 1998 by the New Tactics in Human Rights program of the Center for Victims of Torture. With additional developments, it has become an important tool within the New Tactics Strategic Effectiveness method for advocacy. For more information on the tactical map tool see www.newtactics.org/toolkit/map-terrain.

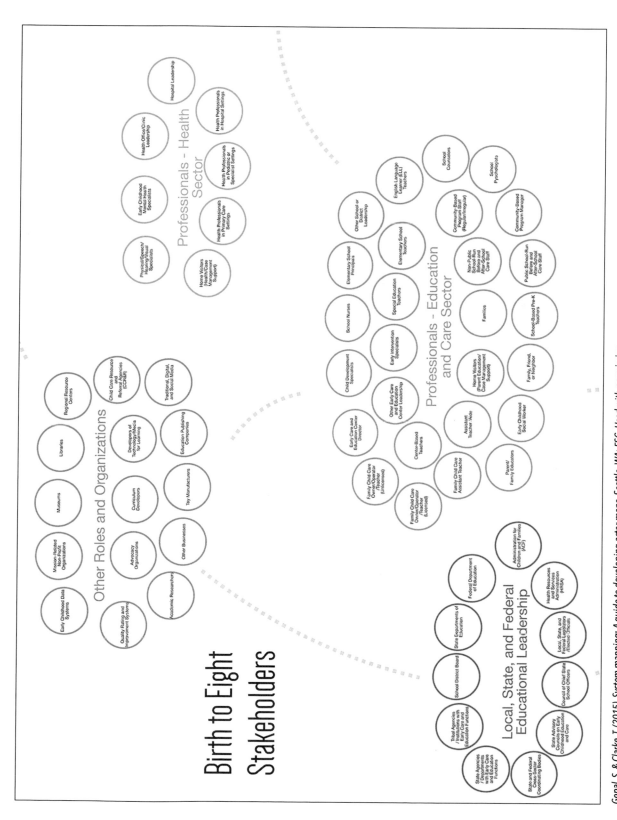

Birth to Eight Stakeholders

Other Roles and Organizations

Early Childhood Data Systems

Mission-Related Non-Profit Organizations

Museums

Libraries

Regional Resource Centers

Quality Rating and Improvement Systems

Academic Research

Advocacy Organizations

Curriculum Developers

Developers of Technology/Media for Learning

Child Care Resource and Referral Agencies (CCR&R)

Other Businesses

Toy Manufacturers

Education Publishing Companies

Traditional, Digital, and Social Media

Professionals – Health Sector

Physical/Speech/ Hearing/Vision Specialists

Early Childhood Mental Health Specialists

Health Office/Clinic Leadership

Hospital Leadership

Health Professionals in Hospital Settings

Health Professionals in Pediatric or Specialist Settings

Health Professionals in Primary Care Settings

Home Visitors (Health/Case Management Support)

Professionals – Education and Care Sector

Child Development Specialists

School Nurses

Elementary School Principals

Other School or District Leadership

English Language Learner (ELL) Teachers

School Counselors

School Psychologists

Early Care and Education Center Director

Other Early Care and Education Center Leadership

Early Intervention Specialists

Special Education Teachers

Elementary School Teachers

Community-Based Program Staff (Regular/Irregular)

Community-Based Program Manager

Family Child Care Owner/Operator /Teacher (Unlicensed)

Center-Based Teachers

Assistant Teacher /Aide

Home Visitors (Parent Education/ Case Management Support)

Families

Non-Public School-Run Before and After-School Care Staff

Public School-Run Before and After-School Care Staff

Family Child Care Owner/Operator /Teacher (Licensed)

Family Child Care Assistant Teacher

Paren/ Family Educators

Early Childhood Social Worker

Family, Friend, or Neighbor

School-Based Pre-K Teachers

Local, State, and Federal Educational Leadership

Tribal Agencies /Institutions with Early Care and Education Functions

School District Board

State Departments of Education

Federal Department of Education

Administration for Children and Families (ACF)

State Agencies /Departments with Early Care and Education Functions

State and Federal Cross-Sector Coordinating Bodies

State Advisory Councils on Early Childhood Education and Care

Council of Chief State School Officers

Local, State, and Federal Legislators /Elected Officials

Health Resources and Services Administration (HRSA)

Gopal, S. & Clarke, T. (2015). System mapping: A guide to developing actor maps. Seattle, WA: FSG. Used with permission.

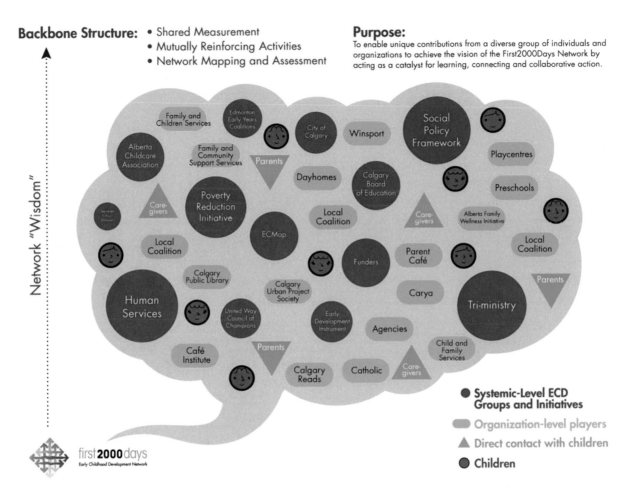

Backbone Structure:
- Shared Measurement
- Mutually Reinforcing Activities
- Network Mapping and Assessment

Purpose:
To enable unique contributions from a diverse group of individuals and organizations to achieve the vision of the First2000Days Network by acting as a catalyst for learning, connecting and collaborative action.

- Systemic-Level ECD Groups and Initiatives
- Organization-level players
- Direct contact with children
- Children

Butler, B., Thomas, R., First 2000 Days Network Backbone Team. (2015). Strategic Development Plan. Used with permission.[24]

System actor maps can identify potential new allies such as different organizations, community champions, or funding bodies. Many of the relationships you identify have the potential to become new supporters. System actor maps can also illuminate new opportunities or strategies for enhancing your sustainability if you consider each connection or "node" in the map as a point of potential intervention. In systems language, we call these Leverage Points. Leverage points are places within the system that can be tweaked in such a way that support greater impact, or in this case, a program sustainability strategy. Note, however, that while some leverage points are easy to adjust and may only need a screwdriver, others may require a power drill.

[24] Note that this map does not intend to illustrate all the actors in the Early Childhood Development System in Calgary, Alberta. Rather, it illustrates different tiers of stakeholders, with some named examples, to bring into focus the purpose and function of the First 2000 Days Network as an entity.

When done as a group, a system actor map can stimulate creative brainstorming around your program's sustainability as well as increase understanding of your issue, challenge assumptions, and promote consensus. If it feels a bit daunting, follow the steps on the next page. Think of it as another way of brainstorming all the different stakeholders that your program has the potential to impact. To be most useful, consider your system actor map as a dynamic picture that continually changes. Revisit it regularly for new insights.

While some leverage points are easy to adjust and may only need a screwdriver, others may require a power drill.

Try It!

Name: System Actor Map
Purpose: To identify new program supporters and sustainability strategies.
Materials: • whiteboard or large piece of mural paper
  • sticky notes
  • markers, crayons, etc.

Steps:

1. Write the name of your program or the issue you are trying to change in the centre of the map and place a circle around it.

2. Ask participants to brainstorm all the people, organizations, or institutions that have an interest, investment, or impact on your program. Record each idea on a sticky note.

Consider Different Actors

• partners
• service providers
• funders
• decision-makers
• clients
• competitors
• people impacted or who can impact

Consider Other Contexts

• policies
• approaches
• supports
• philosophies or principles
• resources
• barriers
• functions
• geographic (local, national, regional, international)
• financial
• political
• social
• current vs. desired

3. Ask participants to add their sticky notes to the map. If necessary, you can rearrange the sticky notes to cluster duplicate or similar ideas together.

4. Begin to identify the relationships present in the system by drawing links between the different actors.

Consider Different Relationships

• positive or negative
• power flows
• competitive
• facilitative

cont'd

Tip

Don't worry about getting the map perfect. Systems mapping is by nature a messy process. If in doubt, get it out and onto the paper. You can change it later.

- formal and informal
- information flows

5. If you choose, you can use different symbols, colours, single or double-ended arrows, thick or thin lines, + or - signs, or solid or dotted lines to describe these actors and the types of relationships between them.

6. When your map is complete, begin to analyze it by posing the following questions to the group for discussion:

- Looking at the system we have drawn, what is the current state of our program's reality? What is the structure that causes this reality?
- Where are the strengths and weaknesses of the system that surrounds our program?
- Where and how can we intervene effectively to change the state of this reality?
- Who can help us to achieve this change?
- Which relationships can result in changes or new policies?
- Which new partners or allies could better support us?
- What must be present to achieve these changes?

- Which key institutions and social groups are currently unaffected by our current strategies?
- Are there any leverage points can we identify?
- Which leverage points can have an impact on many, but are not affected by many, i.e. more powerful and easier to affect?
- What new strategies might be used to engage the areas currently unaffected?
- What is within and outside of our control?
- Which priorities will most likely impact our ability to meet population or individual client needs?

7. Record these insights. You will use them to develop your sustainability strategies in a process described in the next chapter.

A system map is a useful method to identify new supporters of your program. Next, I'll demonstrate a structured process that will tie all of your previous work into a cohesive sustainability strategy.

Chapter 9
SUMMARY

- A system actor map is a useful tool for illustrating the broader relationships that surround your program and identifying new allies who might support you.

- Leverage points in a system actor map can also indicate new opportunities or strategies for enhancing your sustainability.

Review

Let's recap what we've accomplished so far. At this point, you've completed several exercises that will inform the development of your sustainability plan. You've:

- assessed your current sustainability using the Program Sustainability Assessment Tool and identified areas where your sustainability potential is strong and areas where it needs work

- examined your funding situation using the Funding Matrix and pinpointed periods of funding instability, levels of in-kind support, as well as others who should be supporting you (but aren't)

- completed the Worst Case Scenario, which simulates a serious funding cut, and decided which aspects of your program you would maintain and which ones you would scale back or discontinue

- drawn a System Actor Map for your program and identified several new potential supporters.

Now it's time to pull the results of these activities together into a more concrete sustainability plan.

Learning Objectives

In this chapter, you will learn:

- To draft concrete strategies for increasing your sustainability.

Chapter 10: Strategizing for Sustainability

Developing Sustainability Strategies

This next activity is again adapted from the Center for Civic Partnerships and asks you to consider the outcomes your program has achieved (or anticipates) as well as possible stakeholders who also share a desire to see these outcomes realized. From here your next step is to brainstorm possible strategies for securing the resources you need to operate from these various stakeholders.

Recall that outcomes are the benefits or changes that result from your program's activities. If you're fortunate to have conducted an outcome evaluation already, you will have documented evidence of these outcomes. If not, it's perfectly fine to list the short, intermediate, and long-term outcomes that you anticipate. You might have identified these already in your program proposal or your program's Logic Model or Theory of Change (if you have one).

If you completed the Worst Case Scenario exercise in Chapter 8 and Systems Map in Chapter 9, you will already have a list of potential new partners and supporters to add to the second column of the Sustainability Strategies Worksheet on page 111. When you examine the first column more closely, you might find additional stakeholders that you've never even considered.

Once you have a complete list of stakeholders, look at each and consider how they might support your program. Could they provide funding or in-kind support, or perhaps additional volunteers? Or is there a program champion in there somewhere? Each of these ideas can translate into a formal sustainability strategy.

Take a look at how two different programs, Bear Aware (see page 47), and an Aboriginal drop-in centre, have approached this exercise.

You'll see that with just a little thought about what outcomes you can achieve, you can expand your list of stakeholders to something much larger than you had before. From there, you can begin to brainstorm new strategies that will move your program closer to sustainability.

Sustainability Strategies Worksheet - Bear Aware

Justification of Support	Stakeholders	Resources Needed	Sustainability Strategies
What outcomes have you achieved (or anticipate) that would justify the continuation of this program to others?	Given these outcomes, to whom is this program important?	What resources are needed to continue?	What are some possible strategies for securing these resources from the stakeholders in the second column?
• increased community awareness • better garbage management • fewer bear-human interactions • less Conservation Officer time spent responding to incidents • fewer bears destroyed • less unsightly trash in public spaces • less municipal employee time spent cleaning up trash • decreased property damage • safer communities • enhanced community reputation • increased tourism • increased civic pride	• BC Ministry of the Environment • BC Conservation Officer Service • local municipalities • regional districts • Chambers of Commerce • Union of BC Municipalities • school administrators • local Conservation Officers • Guide Outfitters Association of BC • Worksafe BC • Northern BC Tourism Association • Wilderness Tourism Association • local eco-tour operators • CP Rail • Greenpeace • other environmental groups • local naturalist groups • local ranchers • individual wildlife biologists • BC Restaurant and Food Services Association • local fast food outlets • BC Hydro • RCMP • local resource-based industries • local wine & fruit growers • local service clubs • local realtors and developers • Communities in Bloom programs • local First Nation bands • local golf course operators • National Golf Course Owners Association, BC Chapter	• salaries & wages • website hosting & management • travel funds • office space • marketing & communications expertise	1. Develop more diversified funding streams from new stakeholders identified. 2. Conduct a province-wide outcome evaluation of the program. 3. Develop a communication plan to promote our successes more widely. 4. Develop a business plan for the sale of bear-proof garbage cans. 5. Identify and nurture more champions in the provincial government. 6. Approach Northern BC Tourism for assistance with promoting our message through their channels. 7. Ask another environmental group for assistance with website hosting and management. 8. Acknowledge our partners better. 9. Open discussions with our host agency about becoming a core program.

Center for Civic Partnerships. (2011). Sustainability toolkit: 10 steps to maintaining your community improvements, 2nd edition. Sacramento, CA: Public Health Institute. Adapted with permission. Available from http://www.civicpartnerships.org.

Survive and Thrive: Three Steps to Securing Your Program's Sustainability

Sustainability Strategies Worksheet – Aboriginal Drop-in Centre

Justification of Support	Stakeholders	Resources Needed	Sustainability Strategies
What outcomes have you achieved (or anticipate) that would justify the continuation of this program to others?	Given these outcomes, to whom is this program important?	What resources are needed to continue?	What are some possible strategies for securing these resources from the stakeholders in the second column?
<ul><li>increased safety for Aboriginal people living on the street</li><li>increased knowledge of services available for Aboriginal people</li><li>increased use of services</li><li>increased awareness of cultural heritage & values</li><li>the rekindling of cultural heritage</li><li>increased sense of Aboriginal unity/belonging</li><li>increased spirituality</li><li>decreased identity crisis</li><li>increased self-esteem</li><li>increased nutrition</li><li>decreased drug & alcohol addiction</li><li>better overall health & wellness</li><li>increased numbers of Aboriginal people leaving the street</li><li>improved prospects for next the generation</li><li>decreased health care costs</li></ul>	<ul><li>First Nations bands</li><li>Aboriginal organizations</li><li>Ministry of Health</li><li>Mental Health Services</li><li>police department</li><li>provincial court services</li><li>local business improvement association</li><li>local businesses</li><li>local tourism association</li><li>Employment & Social Development Canada</li><li>arts councils</li><li>local churches</li><li>local foundations</li><li>HIV/AIDS organizations</li></ul>	<ul><li>operating funds</li><li>staff salaries</li><li>centre volunteers</li><li>program funds</li><li>food supplies</li><li>storage space</li><li>kitchen space</li><li>freezer</li><li>outreach volunteers</li><li>public phone line</li><li>office supplies</li><li>program supplies</li><li>vehicle</li><li>website hosting & management</li></ul>	1. Research where similar Aboriginal organizations receive their funding. 2. Prioritize new stakeholders identified and initiate discussions on how they might support us. 3. Seek more in-kind donations of food, coffee, and other program supplies. 4. Identify and nurture a champion(s). 5. Promote our uniqueness as the only Aboriginal drop-in space in our community. 6. Hold an Open House and invite potential funders, partners, and the media to attend. 7. Approach media outlets to do a story on how we address drug & alcohol addiction through reclaiming our cultural heritage. 8. Draft several client success stories. 9. Design and post a distinctive poster at other service providers. 10. Recruit a volunteer communications professional from new stakeholders to develop a formal communications plan. 11. Entice other service providers to partner with us because of our unique storefront location. 12. Explore the feasibility of renting out our space after hours to other groups. Promote the space as a meeting room or for board and staff retreats. 13. Explore offering fee-for-service bannock making classes, carving classes, and educational tours for tourists, foreign language students, etc. 14. Find a graduate student interested in conducting a process and outcome evaluation.

Center for Civic Partnerships. (2011). Sustainability toolkit: 10 steps to maintaining your community improvements, 2nd edition. Sacramento, CA: Public Health Institute. Adapted with permission. Available from http://www.civicpartnerships.org.

Try It!

Name: Strategizing for Sustainability

Purpose: To brainstorm new sustainability strategies based on your anticipated outcomes and new stakeholders.

Materials: • Sustainability Strategies Worksheet

• projector and screen

Steps:

1. As a group, brainstorm anticipated or achieved outcomes from your program. Again I find that projecting the worksheet onto a screen greatly helps to facilitate discussion. Place these outcomes in the "Justification of Support" column.

2. In the "Stakeholders" column, brainstorm all the individuals, groups, and institutions you can think of that might share a similar desire to see these same outcomes realized. It's important that you list actual groups or entities instead of generic terms like "parents" or "the community" as you might want to approach them later. You may wish to include some of the new stakeholders you discovered during the Worst Case Scenario exercise in Chapter 8 or the System Map you developed in Chapter 9.

3. In the "Resources Needed" column, determine the resources that you need to continue. In addition to funding, don't forget to include in-kind items such as program space, volunteers, materials and supplies, or professional expertise in areas like marketing or communications.

4. In the "Sustainability Strategies" column, brainstorm possible strategies for securing these resources from the list of stakeholders in Column 2. Don't forget to incorporate any other ideas that may have arisen during the other exercises you completed previously: the Program Sustainability Assessment Tool, the Funding Matrix, Worst Case Scenario, and System Map.

Tip

The longer you brainstorm, the more creative your group's thinking will be and the more innovative the ideas that emerge. For this exercise, set aside an hour or more. For more brainstorming tips check out the ideas on the next page.

5. Transfer these strategies into the first column of the Sustainability Action Plan Worksheet in Chapter 12.

Tips

Here are several tips to help you get the most from your brainstorming.

1. Ask participants to individually brainstorm on the desired topic several days in advance of the group session to jumpstart their thinking.

2. Create a safe atmosphere where participants feel comfortable sharing their diverse knowledge and ideas. Avoid commenting on participants' ideas, positive or negative. Judging, rating or ranking ideas can intimidate others and prevent them from contributing.

3. If there are power imbalances in the room it might make it hard for everyone to speak up. Consider starting by giving everyone several sticky notes of the same color. Ask them to legibly write down one idea per sticky note. Give participants five minutes to use as many sticky notes as they want. Ask participants to stick them to a wall where everyone can then review and discuss.

4. A good brainstorming session is one where people blend and improve upon one another's ideas in a synergistic way. If you've successfully created the atmosphere above, this will be more likely to occur.

5. Go for as long as you can. The first few minutes of any brainstorm usually elicit ideas that are at the forefront of people's minds and aren't particularly creative. This is followed by a lull when all ideas seem to be exhausted. But if you can keep participants in place longer (even though it may seem uncomfortable), you'll start to see significantly more innovative ideas emerge after the 35-minute mark.

6. Consider using a professional facilitator if you don't have anyone with good facilitation skills in-house.

In this chapter I presented a systematic process for brainstorming innovative and concrete sustainability strategies from an expanded list of potential supporters. In the next chapter we'll look at program champions and the critical role that they play in this area.

Chapter 10
SUMMARY

- Strategizing for Sustainability is a group activity that uses your program's documented or anticipated outcomes as a basis for brainstorming new and existing stakeholders who also share a desire to see these outcomes achieved.

- Having an expanded list of supporters enables you to begin crafting possible strategies for securing the operating resources you need from these various stakeholders.

Learning Objectives

In this chapter, you will learn:

- To identify new champions to support your program.

Chapter 11: Identifying Program Champions

In Chapter 3, we talked about the critical role that program champions play in increasing your program's sustainability. However, recruiting these individuals is not a hit-or-miss activity. Take a look at the example below to see how you can consciously identify and recruit appropriate champions in a more strategic and effective manner.

Champions Identification Worksheet

Program	Potential Champion	Common Interest	Best Argument for Their Involvement	How to Get Them Involved	Who Should Initially Approach
Youth Literacy Program	John Smith, bookstore manager	His son benefited from this program	Young people who can read are future customers	Invite to a short goal-setting session	The program tutor who worked with his son last semester
Seniors Program	June Simms, local bank president	Many seniors are customers of her bank	Program has access to 200 seniors who might join her bank	Ask her to comment briefly on strategic plan for the next quarter	A senior in the program who is a retired banker
Environmental Program for 10th Graders	Jack Finch, local nursery owner	Greater appreciation for beautifying yards & public spaces	More youth and parents who will frequent nursery	Ask to review plan for semester & suggest ways to improve it	Student's mom who is owner of three rental properties that were landscaped using Jack's nursery
Child Immunization Project	Jackie Woo, regional director of a pharmaceutical company	Improved health of children	Positive publicity for firm	Ask for ideas for marketing campaign	Retired doctor who volunteers part-time for the program

Hailman, S. (2001). *Building sustainability into your program. Retrieved from http://www.nationalserviceresources.org. Adapted with permission.*

Don't forget that your program champion is usually a busy person. They like your program and feel passionate about what you do, but they have many things on the go and may not have enough time to sit on the board of your organization.

Also, keep in mind that staff typically do not make good champions. While this obviously depends on the organization, employees do not usually have access to the higher-level connections and resources that an external champion would. People also view staff as having a vested interest in continuing the program, versus someone external to the organization. I believe that it's the voluntary and arm's length nature of an external champion's efforts that creates the powerful influence on your sustainability. The only instance where this might not be true is if you work within a large organization or institution. In this case, the endorsement from a champion at the senior executive level can be very effective in determining if your program will continue.

Staff typically do not make good champions.

A Tale of Two Champions
Gibsons Public Market

When Gibsons Public Market volunteers, Nick Sonntag and Gerry Zipursky, saw a former yacht club building on the harbour sitting vacant for ten years, they envisioned a year-round community hub and meeting place where people could buy local produce, enjoy arts and entertainment, and connect with other community members. They also saw the potential to create a learning centre which would provide a marine education centre, community kitchen, and community meeting space. This dream is now a reality, and it is clear that the personal qualities of these two champions played an enormous role in the market's creation. To begin, both men brought a wealth of experience and capability to the endeavour. As an environmental leader on the international stage, Nick worked alongside world leaders as the Canadian Chief of Staff for the 1992 Rio Earth Summit, plus other stints with the UN and other environmental institutions. This gave him not only the experience but also the confidence to embrace the project's vision and inspire others in turn. With a strong background in leadership and community development, Gerry also had the skills to engage with various sectors to make it happen. When it came time to recruit members to the Board, both were aware that the CEO of TELUS, a large Canadian corporation, owned property in the area. They were comfortable recruiting him as an Honorary Chair for their Board of Governors, which also led to a major partnership with TELUS. Along with this confidence came the connections necessary to take the project to the next level. Gerry already sat on the municipal planning commission and Nick had an impressive collection of contacts from his previous work. They were able to use these connections to engage and leverage the participation of others in the project which resulted in additional partnerships with the municipality and several Canadian financial institutions. People describe Nick as being a great communicator with a "magnetic personality." This was an important skill as they reached out to 1500 people in the community regarding the project. Gerry credits their success in recruiting over 300 volunteers to their ability to stay the course and their commitment to building a stronger and healthier community. He says, *"If you can't lead by example you can't get people to follow you."* No matter how far their work may have taken them into the world, the Gibsons Public Market is a project that fired their enthusiasm close to home. *"What really convinced people was our passion and excitement,"* he says. *"Most got involved because they felt good about the collective energy and positive spirit of the project."* In two and a half short years, they were able to generate over $3 million to establish a capital campaign, purchase the property, and begin renovations to the building, which is no minor accomplishment. Although Nick passed away suddenly in 2015, the role these two champions have played in creating this legacy for the community will not be forgotten.

Cultivating a Program Champion

Once you've identified some potential champions, your next step is to carefully nurture the relationship. If you've completed the Champions Identification worksheet, you'll likely have some strategies in mind. Here are a few other ideas to help you with this important step.

- Research in advance their interests and history. What organizations have they supported in the past and how? Where have they worked previously?

- Meet with the person tasked with making the initial approach and develop a game plan. Look for ways that your program might intersect with their interests. In what ways can your effort further their personal goals and objectives?

- Make the ask. Be clear about what you are asking the champion to do and the time involved.

Once your champions are on board:

- Give them clear but appropriate tasks given their time limitations. For example, do you want them to present to your local city, or arrange a meeting with a key policy maker?

- Keep them informed by providing regular, personal updates on the status and accomplishments of your program. Make sure they can speak clearly and correctly about your program's goals and successes.

- If they are a past client (for example a parent), what do they need to feel comfortable in the role of a champion? How are their public speaking skills? How comfortable are they in educating decision-makers about the importance of your program? If necessary, suggest key messages for them to convey or give them talking points. Ensure they are aware of any confidentiality or privacy considerations they need to keep in mind when talking about other clients.

- Look for opportunities to recognize them and their contribution publicly. For example, can you mention them on your website, give them an award, or invite them to events involving the media?

Don't forget, program champions are one of the strongest factors associated with your program's sustainability. However, note that any negative publicity surrounding your champion does have the potential of rubbing off on your program. So do your research and choose wisely. You won't regret it.

You now have a highly useful tool for strategically identifying potential program champions. In the following chapter, I'll introduce you to one last activity that fosters action and accountability for your entire sustainability plan.

Try It!

Name: Identifying Program Champions
Purpose: To strategically identify potential program champions and ways of recruiting and cultivating their initial involvement.
Materials: Identifying Program Champions Worksheet

Steps:
1. Place participants into small groups of approximately four people. Provide each group with a blank worksheet.

2. Give them 20 to 30 minutes to complete as many lines in the worksheet as they can.

3. Debrief in the large group.

Tip

Avoid the temptation to aim too high for champions, such as local celebrities. Although famous people do indeed champion causes and charities, you are better investing your time in nurturing a more accessible, local individual who is connected at a level that can provide you with more immediate and tangible benefits.

Chapter II
SUMMARY

- Program champions play a significant role in promoting program longevity. The voluntary and arm's length nature of their efforts creates a powerful influence on your sustainability.

- Program champions should be recruited, engaged, and managed via a thoughtful and strategic approach that respects their personal passions and busy schedule.

Step 3 - Implement

Have you ever left a meeting where people raised lots of good ideas but nobody ever took action on them? Did you ever wonder where those ideas go? I know. They float up into the ether just above the meeting room ceiling. I've been in those kinds of meetings too. It drives me crazy. I hate the idea of great ideas floating away or being captured in reports that gather dust on someone's shelf.

Imagine that at this point you've held your sustainability planning retreat, and you're feeling pretty good about what was accomplished. Now what? In this third and final step, I will show you another worksheet that is critical for ensuring your strategies are implemented, along with some ideas for moving the process along.

Learning Objectives

In this chapter, you will learn:

- To draft an action plan for implementing your sustainability strategies.

Chapter 12: Sustainability Action Plan

Why another plan? The purpose of a sustainability action plan is to take your proposed sustainability strategies and foster accountability. A solid action plan will increase the likelihood of follow-through and help you to monitor your progress. On the following page is a sustainability action plan I developed with Bear Aware staff. Note the strategies in the "Sustainability Strategies" column are lifted directly from the last column of the Bear Aware Sustainability Strategies Worksheet in Chapter 10.

There are a couple of things I particularly like about using this format for an action plan.

- Each sustainability strategy is broken down into several manageable tasks.
- Each task is assigned to a particular person or group.
- Each task has a deadline for completion.
- Responsibility for tasks is spread among more than one person.
- Resources required are clearly specified.

Notice in particular the sections in red. These are items that were filled in by the group after the main sustainability planning session. They weren't able to complete the entire action plan at the session, but it's a great indicator of all that a group can accomplish during this time. Frankly, I'm always a bit skeptical of action plans developed at the end of a long day of planning. I recommend scheduling a follow up meeting one week later to develop concrete implementation steps.

Sustainability Action Plan Worksheet – Bear Aware[25]

Sustainability Strategy (from Chapter 10)	Specific Tasks	Person(s) Responsible	Time Frame	Resources Required	✓
1. Develop more diversified funding streams from new stakeholders identified.	Identify potential sponsors and obtain Board approval.	Francis with John and Adrienne	June		
	Contact fundraising consultants to get cost estimates.	Pierre	March		
	Apply for an EnviroPOD grant to hire a fundraising consultant.	Pierre	March		
	Apply to Board for funds to hire a fundraising consultant.	Salim & Adrienne			
	Investigate becoming a membership organization.	Part of business plan	July		
	Conduct a review of how we currently fund communities wanting this program.	PAC			
2. Conduct a province-wide outcome evaluation of the program.	Source funds from the Ministry of the Environment.	Francis	July		
	Collate EnviroCorps report data.	Pierre	March (upon approval of the Board)		
	Develop a program logic model [start by email in January].	Adrienne with Francis, John, and Pierre	July		
3. Develop a communication plan to promote our successes more widely.	Send a letter with a Bear Aware t-shirt to the Minister of the Environment.	Adrienne (Zhang to confirm who sends letter)	March (upon approval of the Board)		
	Develop an overall communications strategy. Include a monthly newsletter to stakeholders and two conference calls per year involving all communities who care to join.	Peter with PAC and Pierre. The newsletter idea needs to be communicated, and someone must take the lead. Adrienne volunteers to start, but someone else needs to take over.			
	Ask Ministry communications staff for assistance with developing/reviewing plan.				
	Determine our true cost-benefit impact and incorporate into communications materials.				

[25] Note that sections in red were added in subsequent group meetings. All names are fictitious.

Sustainability Strategy (from Chapter 10)	Specific Tasks	Person(s) Responsible	Time Frame	Resources Required	✓
4. Develop a business plan for the sale of our bear-proof garbage cans.	Find and consult with other organizations our size who sell merchandise.	Adrienne and Francis	June		
	Seek grant for assistance with developing business plan.	Adrienne and Francis	August		
	Develop business plan.	Pierre & consultant	December		
	Determine feasibility and decide.	Adrienne, Francis, John, Zhang and Pierre	March		
5. Identify and nurture more champions in the provincial government.	Identify and approach senior staff in the Ministry of the Environment as potential champions.	Adrienne with Francis, John, Zhang and Pierre	July		
	Identify one or more champions from outside government and approach them.	Adrienne	July		
	Produce a case study documenting successful communities and place on Bear Aware and Ministry websites.		March		
6. Approach Northern BC Tourism for assistance with promoting our message through their channels.	Schedule and prepare presentation.	Pierre	November		
7. Ask another environmental group for assistance with website hosting and management.	Brainstorm possible organizations.	Adrienne, Francis, John, Zhang and Pierre	March		
8. Acknowledge our partners better.	Prepare a win-win proposal strategy.	Pierre	April		
	Approach organizations.	Adrienne & Pierre	May		
	Send formal letters of appreciation to partners.	Pierre	December		
	Acknowledge our partners during public presentations and in reports.	All	ongoing		

Your action plan might take weeks, months, or even years to implement, and that's okay. If you started thinking about sustainability early enough, you'll have some breathing room.

You might also choose to fold sections of your action plan into your program or organization's larger strategic plan.

What Else Can You Do to Encourage Implementation?

Developing a sustainability action plan is a great start, but there are other things you can do to help move the implementation along.

1. Consider striking a temporary working group to get things moving.

2. Colour code each task on the action plan according to its deadline. For example, give all tasks coming due in the next six months one colour, those in the next year another colour, and so on. This makes it easy to focus on priorities.

3. Make "Sustainability Planning" a regular agenda item at staff meetings to keep it on everyone's radar.

4. Print everyone a colour copy of the action plan and have them bring it to every meeting for immediate reference.

Reflecting on Your Progress

Consider going back and reassessing your program with the Program Sustainability Assessment Tool to chart your progress every year or so. In the chart on the opposite page, recall how the area in blue represents your initial scores and the area in red indicates how you may have improved over time in each dimension. In what areas have you progressed? Which ones need more effort or a different strategy? This is a good way to validate your efforts and build staff morale.

Changes in Sustainability Capacity Over Time

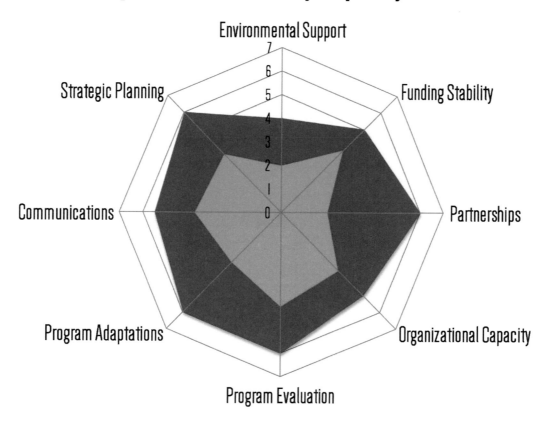

Try It!

Name: Sustainability Action Plan
Purpose: To assist with the timely follow-though of sustainability strategies.
Materials: Sustainability Action Plan Worksheet

Steps:

1. Review all the activities and worksheets you've completed so far: Program Sustainability Assessment Tool, Funding Matrix, Worst Case Scenario, System Map, and Sustainability Strategies. Determine which specific strategies you wish to include in your action plan. Consider carefully which ones you have the capacity to take on.

2. In a large group, place single sheets of flip chart paper horizontally on the wall around the room. The number of sheets should correspond to the number of sustainability strategies you plan to address. Draw four columns on each sheet and label each column with:

   - Sustainability Strategy
   - Specific Tasks
   - Person(s) Responsible
   - Time Frame
   - Resources Required

3. Divide the total number of participants by the number of sheets. This will give you an idea of how many participants to place in each small group. It's best to have three to five in a group maximum.

4. Assign each group one sustainability strategy to start. Instruct them to write the strategy in the first column and then begin to complete the other columns as much as possible. There may be many tasks associated with a strategy or only a few.

5. After 5 to 10 minutes, ask the groups to rotate to the next sheet. Instruct them to review the work of the previous group and add or revise any content they think necessary using a different colour marker.

Tip

At this point you probably think I'm going to recommend a large group debrief, but I'm not. In my experience, people are tired at this point and don't wish to sit through one more debrief. A better strategy is to end the session and have someone type up the flip charts into a document that participants can review at a later time with fresh eyes.

6. Type up the plan and circulate hard copies to participants.

7. Schedule sufficient time at the next staff meeting to review, revise, and complete as necessary.

You now have a technique for ensuring your sustainability strategies translate into a formal action plan. In the next chapter, we'll examine the role that funders can play in promoting sustainability.

Chapter 12
SUMMARY

- A sustainability action plan is an effective way to encourage and monitor implementation of your proposed sustainability strategies.

- Although you might begin to draft a sustainability action plan at the end of your sustainability planning retreat or session, the best time to complete it is at a following meeting when participants are rested and fresh.

- Other tips to facilitate follow-through of your sustainability action plan are to strike a temporary working group and to make sustainability planning a regular agenda item at staff meetings.

Learning Objectives

In this chapter, you will learn:

- The role that funding bodies can play in promoting program sustainability.

Chapter 13: How Funders Can Help with Program Sustainability

Often when I present workshops on program sustainability, someone in the audience will laugh and say, *"I wish our funders appreciated that!"* As stewards of donor and public funds, funding bodies such as government, foundations, and corporate sponsors must be accountable for how they spend money. They also desire beneficial long-term outcomes and a social return on their investment. But how many of these outcomes disappear when seed money disappears? While it is common for grant applications to ask how new programs will sustain themselves post-funding, there is more to fostering sustainability than an open-ended question on an application form.

Throughout this book, I have discussed concrete steps you can take to increase your program's potential for longevity. In this chapter, I'm going to focus on several ways that funders can help. Consider talking frankly with them about the following.

Sustainability Doesn't Arise From Short-term Funding

Traditional one-year funding cycles are effective at keeping program staff busy – looking for other funding, that is. This constant search diverts attention away from not only service delivery but also other critical activities that strengthen sustainability, such as developing partnerships or building community support. Consistent financial support helps a grantee move through all the life cycles of a program: from the pilot phase to the achievement of outcomes, refinement and broader dissemination, and finally large-scale social change. Consider funding cycles that are longer than one year, i.e. three to five years. If funders are nervous about longer funding cycles, they might consider tiered funding levels for multi-year grants to ensure the capacity to continue is present, or incorporating more concrete milestones and deliverables into funding contracts.

Most Outcomes Don't Arise From Short-term Funding

In my experience, the sort of outcomes that funders are typically looking for do not usually appear within the first year of a new program. In fact, intermediate outcomes can often take three to five years (or longer) to appear, and clearly attributable long-term outcomes might never appear. Most community programs are intervening in complex social, behavioural, and environmental issues that can take years to address. Furthermore, the first year of a program is often spent on operational activities such as setting up administration, hiring staff, forming partnerships, building trust, and delivering early programming. While program managers would love to see an immediate impact from their efforts, this is often unreasonable to expect. Funders should discuss with grantees what a reasonable timeline for achieving outcomes would be.

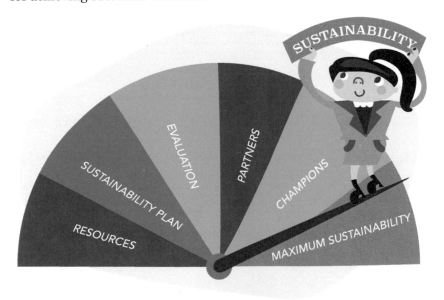

There is a Minimum Threshold For Achieving Sustainability

If you've reached this point in the book, you've likely realized that enhanced sustainability is largely related to areas traditionally associated with nonprofit capacity-building. Factors such as strong leadership, community engagement, and evaluation all play a role in helping programs to thrive. But building this capacity can require significant time and resources. If a new program lacks the resources to fund their actual overhead, staff will often struggle to reach the threshold necessary for sustainability. In fact, in one well-known study, researchers concluded that many health promotion efforts fail to become sustainable because insufficient resources were provided to cover the real program costs over too short a funding period.[26] Both funders and grantees need to be more realistic about the true costs of a program and budget accordingly.

Delays in Funding Impact More Than Program Operations

If programs experience significant delays in receiving revenue, they risk losing talented staff, institutional memory, key partnerships, public trust, and much, much, more. The costs of putting a program on hold only to re-start it several months later are both tangible and intangible, creating immense inefficiencies in the nonprofit sector. Government and other funders should provide multi-year contract funding in a seamless manner.

Don't Ignore the Tried and True

Sometimes it seems like funders are more interested in supporting new and novel pilot projects rather than those that have already proven themselves effective. While ongoing innovation is beneficial, new pilots can often displace yesterday's success story. Eventually, many of these pilots turn into mature programs that struggle themselves to secure sustainable funding. As the noted sustainability researcher, Mary Ann Scheirer, questions:

> Is it ethical for funders to develop innovative programs but then expect others to sustain them if they prove effective?[27]

Traditional one-year funding cycles are effective at keeping program staff busy – looking for other funding, that is.

It's painful to watch initiatives that have innovated, learned, revised, and eventually evolved into effective interventions over time continue to battle funding insecurity. Don't ignore the tried-and-true program in favour of the fresh-and-new pilot. Funders might consider "niche funding" where they stay the course and realize greater long-term impacts.

[26] Goodman, R. M., McLeroy, K. R., Steckler, A. B., & Hoyle, R. H. (1993). Development of level of institutionalization scales for health promotion programs. Health Education Quarterly, 20(2), 161-178.
[27] Scheirer, M. A. & Dearing, J. W. (2011). An agenda for research on the sustainability of public health programs. American Journal of Public Health, 101(11), 2059-2067.

Self-sufficiency is Unrealistic for Most Nonprofits

Vu Le probably summed it up best when he said,

> The concept of sustainability is ubiquitous, overbearing, and frustrating. "Sustainability" is confused with "self-sufficiency," leading grant makers and donors to believe that if nonprofits just try hard enough, they'll reach this state of funding nirvana whereby they can generate their own revenues and never have to bother a foundation again. And if they're not actively working toward reaching fiscal enlightenment, they shouldn't be supported. Here's the issue: this magical land of non-profit financial self-sufficiency does not exist, and the unwillingness of grant makers to admit this perpetuates an inefficient funding system that stymies nonprofits' abilities to tackle society's most challenging problems.[28]

What else can funders do? Here are some additional ideas:

- Educate grant applicants and their grantees on the importance of sustainability planning.

- Provide support for staff and board training in program sustainability.

- Require all grant applicants to complete the Program Sustainability Assessment Tool.

- Allocate small grants that encourage programs to prepare a sustainability plan and implement their sustainability strategies.

- Ask grantees how you can further support their sustainability efforts before funding ends.

We have seen how funders can indeed play a role in promoting program sustainability. All that remains now is your resolve to act.

[28] Le, V. (May 2015). Tough love that doesn't work. Chronicle of Philanthropy, 27(9), 37.

A Funder's View

The Oregon Community Foundation

The Oregon Community Foundation (OCF) is a statewide community foundation with a mission to improve the lives of all Oregonians through the power of philanthropy. I invited Kathleen Cornett, VP of Grants & Programs, and Sonia Worcel, VP of Strategy & Research, to comment on the issue of program sustainability from their perspective as funders.

At the Oregon Community Foundation, we believe that community vitality is strengthened by short term resident-led projects and by strong, sustaining nonprofit organizations. We aim to foster both. Organizations committed to long-term change need to engage in thoughtful sustainability planning, ideally from the outset of program development and grant-seeking.

We encourage and support this work in a number of ways:

- Like most foundations, our applications typically include a question about how organizations will sustain or build on the work they accomplish through our grants. We ask this as a starting point for discussion; we are not looking for a definitive exit strategy. We are exploring whether or not the applicant organization, including the board of directors, is actively engaged in sustainability planning.

- We fund organizational capacity building through multi-year grants, again looking for evidence of careful planning and top-to-bottom commitment to the plans within the organization. Many of these projects intend specifically to build fundraising capacity; we explore sustainable outcomes with the applicant to help them develop realistic, "sticky" goals.

- OCF has worked with other funders, including governmental agencies, to provide long-term funding for existing, effective programming. For example, our participation on the Oregon Parenting Education Collaborative has provided support for regional parenting education hubs for over a decade. That said, foundations cannot be expected to provide ongoing support indefinitely. For many of us, piloting, testing, and exploring the edges of new approaches is also a part of our mission. But we do acknowledge the need to do it responsibly and not chase innovation for innovation's sake.

- OCF also has several five-year initiatives underway, each intended to support organizational capacity building and program sustainability. For example, our out-of-school time grantees are engaging with a program quality improvement framework that strengthens programs and builds staff capacity. Another arts education initiative deliberately encourages communities to experiment (using evaluation to inform evolution and adaptation) until they find an approach that their community can sustain.

As a funder, we feel it is important to recognize that community organizations are the best at understanding their own community's needs and setting their own organizational goals. It is our job to listen, provide support, and continually check our own expectations with regard to organizational capacity and program sustainability. We encourage nonprofit organizations to engage in open conversations with their funders about sustainability, and for other funders to thoughtfully consider their own expectations with regard to sustainability (either perceived or real) of the organizations they fund.

Chapter 13
SUMMARY

- Funders can also play a role in promoting sustainability.

- Through actions such as extending grant cycles beyond one year, ensuring new pilots receive sufficient seed funding, resourcing mature programs, educating grantees, and supporting sustainability plan development, funders of all shapes and sizes can work together with grantees to increase their potential for sustainability.

Conclusion

Now is a good time to look back and revisit all that we've covered. If you've followed the three steps of Assess, Plan, and Implement, you will have:

- assessed your program's current sustainability capacity
- identified periods of potential future funding instability
- prioritized what parts of your program you would save if your funding was drastically cut
- developed concrete strategies for increasing your sustainability
- entered these strategies into a formal sustainability action plan.

Whew! That's a lot of work. Congratulations on making this important investment! Here's how to make sure it pays off in the long run.

Moving Forward

What's left is to remain diligent in keeping sustainability on your agenda and bring your strategies to fruition. As we discussed in Chapter 2, the payoff for your program is huge.

Sustainability Benefits

Remember all the benefits of greater program sustainability:

- less time spent on fundraising, more on service delivery
- freedom to spend resources exactly where needed
- ability to fine-tune activities over time
- achievement of intermediate and longer-term goals
- forward movement on your mission
- greater credibility with stakeholders
- more stable and talented staff
- strong organizational memory
- mutually-beneficial partnerships.

So what are you waiting for? Take charge of your sustainability today and watch your program not only survive, but thrive!

Connect

If you want to learn more, you can find a link to more sustainability resources at: **www.pinterest.com/evaluationmaven/program-sustainability-planning**.

Do you have a sustainability story to share? Contact me at **www.communitysolutions.ca.** I'd love to hear from you!

Bibliography

Afterschool Alliance. (2007). *Designing a sustainability plan*. Retrieved from http://www.afterschoolalliance.org.

Altarum Institute. (2009). *Literature review: Defining sustainability of federal programs based on the experiences of the DHHS Office on Women's Health Multidisciplinary Health Models for Women*. Retrieved from http://www.womenshealth.gov/pub/owh/sustainability- review.pdf.

American Lung Association. (n.d.). *Assessing your clinic's level of institutionalization: Sustainability of clinic-based systems change efforts*. Retrieved from http://www.chcs.org/usr_doc/Medica_and_ALA_Sustainability_Tool.pdf.

Askell-Williams, H., Slee, P., and Van Deur, P. (2013). *Social and emotional wellbeing programs: The nexus between sustainability and quality assurance*. Retrieved from http://hdl.handle.net/2328/27059.

Backer, T. E. (1995). *Dissemination & utilisation strategies for foundations*. Kansas City, MO: Ewing Marion Kauffman Foundation.

Bamberger, M., & Cheema, S. (1990). *Case studies of project sustainability: Implications for policy and operations from Asian experience*. Washington, DC: The World Bank.

Beery, W. L., Senter, S., Cheadle, A., Greenwald, H. P., Pearson, D., Brousseau, R., and Nelson, G. D. (2005). Evaluating the legacy of community health initiatives: A conceptual framework and example from the California Wellness Foundation's Health Improvement Initiative. *American Journal of Evaluation*, 26, 150-165.

Berendsen, B., Kremers, S., Savelberg, H., Schaper, N., & Hendriks, M. (2015). The implementation and sustainability of a combined lifestyle in primary care: Mixed method process evaluation. *BMC Family Practice*, 16, 37.

Bracht, N., Finnegan, J., Rissel, C., Weisbrod, R., Gleason, J., Corbett, J., &

Veblen-Mortenson, S. (1994). Community ownership and program continuation following a health demonstration project. *Health Education Research*, 9(2), 243-255.

Center for Civic Partnerships. (2011). *Sustainability toolkit: 10 steps to maintaining your community improvement*, 2nd edition. Sacramento, CA: Public Health Institute.

Centre for Community Leadership and Grantham, B. (2000). *An examination of project sustainability*. Vancouver, BC: Vancouver Foundation.

Centre for Research and Education in Human Services & Social Planning Council of Cambridge and North Dumfries. (2004). *Building sustainable nonprofits: The Waterloo region experience*. Retrieved from http://www.socialplanningcouncil-cnd.org/pdfs/sustainability_final.pdf.

Coalition for Community Schools. (2016). *Sustainable community schools: A proven approach*. Retrieved from http://www.communityschools.org.

Community-Campus Partnerships for Health. (n.d.). *Self-assessment tool for service-learning sustainability*. Retrieved from http://www.tufts.edu/talloiresnetwork/downloads/service-learningsustainabilitytool.pdf.

Corporation for National & Community Service. (n.d.). *Toolkit for program sustainability, capacity building, and volunteer recruitment/management*. Retrieved from http://www.womenshealth.gov/owh/pub/sustainability-review.cfm.

Crone, M., Verlaan, M., Willemsen, M., Soelen, P. V., Reijneveld, S., Sing, R. H., Paulussen, T. (2006). Sustainability of the prevention of passive infant smoking within well-baby clinics. *Health Education & Behavior*, 33(2), 178-196.

Cummings, R., & McConney, A. (2008, September). *Evaluating sustainability in public programs*. Roundtable paper presented at the Australasian Evaluation Society 2008 International Conference.

Retrieved from http://researchrepository.murdoch.edu.au/10289/.

Doyle, C., Howe, C., Woodcock, T., Myron, R., Phekoo, K., McNicholas, C., Saffer, J., & Bell, D. (2013). Making change last: Applying the NHS Institute for Innovation and Improvement sustainability model to healthcare improvement. *Implementation Science*, 8, 127.

Dubois, N., Kisby, M. (1999). *Heart health sustainability: Workbook for action*. Toronto, ON: Ontario Public Health Association.

Duplechain, M. (2001). *Sustainability means more than money!* The Resource Connection, 4(2). Retrieved from http://www.nationalserviceresources.org.

Evashwick, C., Ory, M. (2003). Organisational characteristics of successful innovative health care programs sustained over time. *Family and Community Health*, 26(3), 177-193.

Feinberg, M., Bontempo, D., & Greenberg, M. (2008). Predictors and level of sustainability of community prevention coalitions. *American Journal of Preventive Medicine*, 34(6), 495-501.

Fleiszer, A., Semenic, S., Ritchie, J., Richer, M., & Denis, J. (2016). A unit-level perspective on the long-term sustainability of nursing best practice guidelines program: An embedded multiple case study. *International Journal of Nursing Studies*, 53, 204-218.

Foreman, R. et al. (2001). *Assessing the sustainability of the "Just Walk It" program model: Is it effective and will it enhance program success?* Paper presented at the Walking the 21st Century: An International Walking Conference, February 20, 2001, Perth, Western Australia.

Gomez, B., Greenberg, M., & Feinberg, M. (2005). Sustainability of community coalitions: An evaluation of communities that care. *Prevention Science*, 6(3), 199-202.

Gonzales, A., Schofield, R., & Hernandez, N. (2005). *Developing a sustainability plan for Weed and Seed sites.* Retrieved from www.ojp.usdoj.gov/ccdo/pub/pdf/ncj210462.pdf.

Goodman, R. M., McLeroy, K. R., Steckler, A. B., & Hoyle, R. H. (1993). Development of level of institutionalization scales for health promotion programs. *Health Education Quarterly,* 20(2), 161-178.

Goodman, R. M., Steckler, A. (1989). A model for the institutionalization of health promotion programs. *Family and Community Health,* 11(4), 63-78.

Goodson, P., Smith, M. M., Evans, A., Meyer, B., & Gottlieb, N. (2001). Maintaining prevention practice: Survival of PPIP in primary care settings. *American Journal of Preventative Medicine,* 20(3), 184-189.

Greenhalgh, T., Robert, G., Bate, P. (2004). *How to spread good ideas: A systematic review of the literature on diffusion, dissemination, and sustainability of innovations in health service delivery and organization.* Report for the National Co-ordinating Centre for NHS Service Delivery and Organisation R & D (NCCSDO). Retrieved from http://www.nets.nihr.ac.uk/projects/hsdr/081201038.

Gruen, R. L., Elliott, J. H., Nolan, M.L., Lawton, P. D., Parkhill, A., McLaren, C.J., Lavis, J.N. (2008). Sustainability science: An integrated approach for health-programme planning. *Lancet,* 372(9649), 1579-1589.

Hailman, S. (2001). *Building sustainability into your program.* Retrieved from http://www.nationalserviceresources.org.

Harris, N., and Sandor, M. (2013). Defining sustainable practice in community-based health promotion: A Delphi study of practitioner perspectives. *Health Promotion Journal of Australia,* 24(1), 53-60.

Hawe, P., King, L., Noort, M., Jordens, C., & Lloyd, B. (2000). *Indicators to help with capacity-building in health promotion.* Retrieved from http://www.health.nsw.gov.au.

Holder, H. D. and Moore, R. S. (2000). Institutionalization of community action projects to reduce alcohol-use related problems: Systematic facilitators. *Substance Use & Misuse,* 35(1&2), 75-86.

Howard, D., & Howard, P. (2000). Towards sustainability of human services: Assessing community self-determination and self-reliance. *Canadian Journal of Program Evaluation,* 15(1), 24-41.

J. W. McConnell Family Foundation. (1998). *Should you sow what you know? The Foundation's primer for those developing, or referring, an applied dissemination proposal.* Montreal, PQ: J. W. McConnell Family Foundation.

Jackson, C., Fortmann, S.P., Flora, J.A., Melton, R.J., Snider, J.P., & Littlefield, D. (1994). The capacity-building approach to intervention maintenance implemented by the Stanford Five-City Project. *Health Education Research,* 9(3), 385-396.

Jansen, M., Harting, J., Ebben, N., Kroon, B., Stappers, J., Engelshoven, E. V., et al. (2008). The concept of sustainability and the use of outcome indicators: A case study to continue a successful health counselling intervention. *Family Practice,* 25, 32-37.

Jobs to Careers National Program Office. (n.d.). *The Jobs to Careers sustainability planning tool.* Retrieved from http://www.jobs2careers.org/pdf/J2C_Sustainability_Tool_092909.pdf.

Johnson, K., Hays, C, Center, H., & and Daley, C. (2004). Building capacity and sustainable prevention innovations: A sustainability planning model. *Evaluation and Program Planning,* 27, 135-49.

Johnston, M. (2004). *Investing in sustainability: Adding value in Georgia.* Retrieved from www.asph.org/UserFiles/Nelson.pdf.

Kafyulilo, A., Fisser, P., and Voogt, J. (2014, March). *Determinants of the sustainability of teacher design teams as a professional development arrangement for developing technology integration knowledge and skills.* Paper presented at the meeting of Society for Information Technology & Teacher Education International Conference, Jacksonville, FL.

Kraft, K., & O'Neill, C. (2007). *Evolutionary sustainability: Reconceptualizing sustainability of organizational and community change.* Retrieved from http://www.wholonomyconsulting.com.

Leger, L. S. (2005). Questioning sustainability in health promotion projects and programs. *Health Promotion International,* 20(4), 317-319.

Lewis, A. (n.d.). *Nonprofit organizational assessment tool.* Retrieved from http://coco-net.org/wp-content/uploads/2012/08/Nonprofit-Organizational-Assessment-Tool.pdf.

Lodl, K., & Stevens, G. (2002). Coalition sustainability: Long-term successes & lessons learned. *Journal of Extension,* 40(1), 1-8.

Luke, D.A., Calhoun, A., Robichaux, C.B., Elliott, M.B., Moreland-Russell, S. (2014). The program sustainability assessment tool: A new instrument for public health programs. *Preventing Chronic Disease,* 11, 130184.

Maher, L., Gustafson, D., & Evans, A. (2010). *Sustainability model and guide.* Retrieved from http://www.institute.nhs.uk/sustainability.

Management Sciences for Health. (2004). *Management and organizational sustainability tool.* Retrieved from http://erc.msh.org/mainpage.cfm?file=95.40.htm&module=toolkit&language=English.

Mancini, J. A., Marek, L. I., & Brock, D. (2003, May). *Sustaining community-based programs for families: Program development implications from longitudinal research*. Research lecture presented at the USDA Children, Youth, and Families at Risk (CYFAR) Annual Meeting, Minneapolis, MN.

Mancini, J., & Marek, L. (2004). Sustaining community-based programs for families: Conceptualization and measurement. *Family Relations*, 53(4), 339-347.

Manning, M., Bollig-Fischer, A., Berry Bobovski, L., Lichtenberg, P., Chapman, R., & Albrecht, T. (2014). Modelling the sustainability of community health networks: Novel approaches for analyzing collaborative organization partnerships across time. *Translational Behavioral Medicine*, 4(1), 46-59.

Marek, L. I., Mancini, J. A., & Brock, D. (1999). *Continuity, success, and survival of community-based projects: The national youth at risk program sustainability study*. Petersburg, VA: Virginia Cooperative Extension.

Marek, L. P., & Mancini, J. (2003). *National state strengthening program sustainability study: Patterns of early sustainability*. Retrieved from http://www.ag.arizona.edu/sfcs/cyfernet/evaluation/StSt_final_10-27-03.pdf.

Marek, L., & Mancini, J. (2007). *Sustaining community-based programs: Relationships between sustainability factors and program results*. Retrieved from http://ag.arizona.edu/sfcs/cyfernet/evaluation/Sustaining_2007_cyfar_pp.pdf.

Mendes, R., Plaza, V., and Wallerstein, N. (2016). Sustainability and power in health promotion: community-based participatory research in a reproductive health policy case study in New Mexico. *Global Health Promotion*, 23(1), 61-74.

O'Neill, C. (2007). *Sustainability: More than a fiction writing contest*. Retrieved from www.wholonomyconsulting.com/docs/sustainability-more-than-fiction.pdf.

O'Loughlin, J., L. Renaud, L. Richard, L. S. Gomez, & Paradis, G. (1998). Correlates of the sustainability of community-based heart health promotion intervention. *Preventive Medicine*, 27, 702-12.

Paine-Andrews, A., Fisher, J. L., Campuzano, M. K., Fawcett, S. B., & Berkley-Patton, J. (2000). Promoting sustainability of community health initiatives: An empirical case study. *Health Promotion Practice*, 1(3), 248-258.

Pallas, S., Minhas, D., Pérez-Escamilla, R., Taylor, L., Curry, L., & Bradley, E. (2013). Community health workers in low- and middle- income countries: What do we know about scaling up and sustainability? *American Journal of Public Health*, 103(7), e74-e82.

Pluye, P., Potvin, L., & Denis, J. (2004). Making public health programs last: Conceptualizing sustainability. *Evaluation and Program Planning*, 27, 121-133.

Proctor, E., Luke, D., Calhoun, A., McMillen, C., Brownson, R., McCrary, S., & Padek, M. (2015). Sustainability of evidence-based healthcare: Research agenda, methodological advances, and infrastructure support. *Implementation Science*, 10, 88.

Reinke, W. (1999). A multi-dimensional program evaluation model: Considerations of cost-effectiveness, equity, quality, and sustainability. *Canadian Journal of Program Evaluation*, 14(2), 145-160.

Ridde, V., Pluye, P., & Johnson-Lafleur, J. (2007). *Sustainability tool kit*. Retrieved from http://www.cacis.umontreal.ca.

Rogers, P., & Williams, B. (2008). *Sustainability of services for young children and their families: What works?* Retrieved from http://www.aracy.org.au.

Rosenheck, R. (2001). Stages in the implementation of innovative clinical programs in complex organisations. *Journal of Nervous and Mental Disease*, 189(12), 812-821.

Sarriot, E., Winch, P., Ryan, L., Bowie, J., Kouletio, M., Swedberg, E., LeBan, K., Edison, J., Welch, R., & Pacqué, M. (2004). A methodological approach and framework for sustainability assessment in NGO-implemented primary health care programs. *International Journal of Health Planning and Management*, 19(1), 23-41.

Savaya, R., Elsworth, G., & Rogers, P. (2008). Projected sustainability of innovative social programs. *Evaluation Review*, 33, 189-205.

Savaya, R., Spiro, S., & and El-ran-Barak, R. (2008). Sustainability of social programs: A comparative case study analysis. *American Journal of Evaluation*, 29, 478-493.

Scheirer, M. A. (2005). Is sustainability possible? A review and commentary on empirical studies of program sustainability. *American Journal of Evaluation*, 26(3), 320-347.

Scheirer, M. A., & Dearing, J. W. (2011). An agenda for research on the sustainability of public health programs. *American Journal of Public Health*, 101(11), 2059-2067.

Scheirer, M. A., & Dearing, J. W. (2013). Linking sustainability research to intervention types. *American Journal of Public Health*, 103(4), e73-e80.

Scheirer, M., Hartling, G., & Hagerman, D. (2008). Defining sustainability outcomes of health programs: Illustrations from an on-line survey. *Evaluation and Program Planning*, 31, 335-346.

Shediac-Rizhallah and Bone, L. R. (1998). Planning for the sustainability of community-based health programs: Conceptual frameworks and future directions for research, practice and policy. *Health Education Research*, 13(1), 87-108.

Schell, S., Luke, D., Schooley, M., Elliott, M., Herbers, S., Mueller, N., et al (2013). Public health program capacity for sustainability: A new framework. *Implementation Science*, 8(15), 1-9.

Shigayeva, A. and Coker, R. (2014). Communicable disease control programmes and health systems: An analytical approach to sustainability. *Health Policy & Planning*, 30(3), 368-385.

Smith, M. Buckwalter, K.C., Zevenbergen, P.W., Kudart, P., Springer-Brenneman, D., & Garand, L. (1993). An administrator's dilemma: Keeping the innovative mental health and aging programs alive after the grant funds end. *Journal of Mental Health Administration*, 20(3), 212-222.

Steckler, A., Goodman, R., McLeroy, K. R., Davis, S., & Koch, G. (1992). Measuring the diffusion of innovative health promotion programs. *American Journal of Health Promotion*, 6(3), 214-225.

Stephenson, R., Tsui, A. O., & Knight, R. (2004). Measuring family planning sustainability at the outcome and programme levels. *Health Policy and Planning*, 19(2), 88-100.

Stirman, S., Kimberly, J., Cook, N., Calloway, A., Castro, F., & Charns, M. (2012). The sustainability of new programs and innovations: A review of the empirical literature and recommendations for future research. *Implementation Science*, 7(17).

Substance Abuse and Mental Health Services Administration (SAMHSA). (2008). *Sustaining grassroots community-based programs: A toolkit for community-and faith-based service providers*. Retrieved from http://www.samhsa.gov.

Swerissen, H., & Crisp, B. (2004). The sustainability of health promotion interventions for different levels of social organization. *Health Promotion International*, 19(1), 123-130.

Taylor, J. (2006). Sustainability on the fly. Folsom, CA: US Dept. of Education Mentoring Resource Centre.

The Community Toolbox. *Toolkits: Sustain the work or initiative*. Retrieved from http://ctb.ku.edu.

The Cornerstone Consulting Group (2002). *End games: The challenge of sustainability*. Retrieved from http://www.jointogether.org/resources/end-games-the-challenge-of.html.

The Finance Project. (2003). *Sustainability self-assessment tool*. Retrieved from http://www.ilj.org/publications/docs/Sustainability_Self_Assessment_Tool.pdf.

The Health Communication Unit, Centre for Health Promotion, University of Toronto. (2001). *Sustainability worksheet package*. Retrieved from http://www.thcu.ca/infoandresources/resource_display.cfm?res_topicID=6.

U.S. Department of Labour Employment and Training Administration. (n.d.). *Moving forward: A sustainability planning guide*. Retrieved from www.doleta.gov/Business/PDF/SustainGuide.pdf.

US Department of Health and Human Services, Substance Abuse and Mental Health Services Administration. (2003). *Sustainability assessment tool: Brief overview of how to use the sustainability self-assessment tool with a system of care community*. Retrieved from www.tapartnership.org/docs/sustainabilityStrategicPlanningTemplate.doc.

US Dept. of Education. (2009). *Classroom, school, district & state level self-assessment tool: Sustaining reading first*. Retrieved from http://www2.ed.gov/programs/readingfirst/support/sustaining.html.

Washington University in St. Louis, Center for Tobacco Policy Research. (2011). *Program sustainability assessment tool*. Retrieved from http://www.sustaintool.org/.

Victorian Government Department of Human Services. (2001). *Evidence-based health promotion: Resources for planning – No. 3 Falls Prevention*. Melbourne, AU: Public Health Division.

Weiss, H., Coffman, J., & Bohan-Baker, M. (2003). Evaluation's role in supporting initiative sustainability. *The Evaluation Exchange*, 4(3), 1-28.

Whelan, J., Love, P., Pettman, T., Doyle, J., Booth, S., Smith, E., & Waters, E. (2014). Cochrane update: Predicting sustainability of intervention effects in public health evidence: identifying key elements to provide guidance. *Journal of Public Health*, 36(2), 347-351.

Wolff, T. (2010). Tools for sustainability. *Global Journal of Community Psychology Practice: Promoting Community Practice for Social Benefit*, 1(1), 40-57.

Wong, D. J., Gilbert, D. J., & Kilburn, L. (2004). *Seeking program sustainability in chronic disease management: The Ontario experience*. Retrieved from http://www.changefoundation.com.

93020615R00082